A Story For

Every Season

Compiled by: James Pressler

i

Previous titles by the New Lenox Writers' Group:

Writers, We

The Place We Call Home

Troubling Times

Memory Lane

A Matter of Faith

All books are available online

To Janet.
So glad to know you.

Marlene

Cover design by James Pressler

Cover artwork by Tina M. Thomas

Printed in Century 12 pt.

DEDICATION

Dedicated to those in our lives who make the time special. Whether time of the day, the year, or our lives, those people make it important.

TITLES & AUTHORS

Contents

ACKNOWLEDGMENTS

Special thanks to Jens Schommer, who volunteered his time and talents to photograph the writers and put a face to their names. Furthermore, we are always grateful for the hospitality of the New Lenox Public Library in providing our group a place to hone our craft, and hopefully produce works worthy of gracing your shelves.

Escape

by Dawn E. Plestina

O pen, dark. Close, dark. No matter with her eyes open or closed she saw the same amount of darkness- no more, no less. Of course, she had the power to simply flip a light switch or even leave the room. As she lay in the darkness wondering what it was like for her mother who could no longer perform these simple acts, sleep would not return.

***

Last fall as her school year started, Dawn visited her mother at Silver Cross Hospital. Joan suffered a complication with an outpatient medical procedure and returned to the hospital to resolve the problem. A weekend turned into a week which then doubled, with no end in sight to the visit.

As Dawn stopped to pick up some food, she noticed she missed a call. The voicemail did not sound particularly ominous. "Hi, this is Susan Atkins, social worker from Silver Cross Hospital. When you have a chance, please call me. Thank you."

Simple, direct. The kind of message Dawn liked to receive. She figured Susan called to help set up transportation from the hospital to Smith Crossing where Mom lived. Before she could return the call, her sister's name popped up on her cell phone screen. Swiping to accept the call, Dawn answered "Hi, Sharon."

"Hey, how's it going?" Sharon began in her usual greeting

style.

"Um, okay, I guess. I bet you're calling about the social worker."

Momentary silence. Not excruciatingly long but noticeable, enough so that Dawn felt a brief twinge of discomfort.

"So I guess you know."

"Know what?" Dawn asked, confused.

"Where are you right now?"

"I'm picking up food."

"Are you driving?" Sharon asked in a motherly tone.

"No, I'm parked. What's up?" Dawn, starting to feel more than a simple twinge of discomfort, wondered about the exact purpose of the call.

"The social worker who called you also phoned me. She told me that Mom's cancer returned."

Dawn paused to consider those words. "The same cancer from 15 years ago?"

"Yes, it metastasized to her lung." When Dawn did not respond, Sharon attempted to offer understanding with, "I know this is not the news any of us expected to hear."

She was right. It had been almost 16 years since the doctors initially diagnosed their mom with cancer- a chondrosarcoma located behind her knee. This led to an amputation at mid-thigh. It took care of the `cancer until a spot (which was not the same type) was found in her lung two years later. Doctors removed the spot and nothing more showed, that is, until now. Her left lung now showed the same cancer that started over a decade ago.

When Dawn realized she must have been reminiscing for quite some time, she blurted, "John's 'Back to School Night' starts soon; I need to get home." Fall was always a busy time of year because of the beginning of school.

"Are you going to tell the kids?"

"Not tonight. I'll wait until I can tell them together."

As Dawn drove home, tears streamed onto her lap while her chest heaved and she let go and cried aloud. As she approached the driveway, she worked to calm herself. Her kids held keen observational skills, and she not only wanted to tell them together, but she didn't want to leave them after she did.

After school the next day, Dawn told Elaine and John the news that Grandma Joan's cancer returned and that she was choosing not to fight it. They ate dinner in silence and then visited Grandma at Silver Cross. With Aunt Sharon and Uncle Bruce there, they talked and joked which lightened the mood. Since the doctors predicted she had from three months to one year left, a representative from a hospice group visited and spoke about the care they provide.

After the representative left, her mom looked Dawn dead in the eyes and said, "I want medical marijuana." She maintained determined eye contact as if to prevent any family member from disagreeing with her. No family member objected to her wish because they all knew how rough chemo was on her physical body and mind, all those years ago. To survive the cancer, she decided on a leg amputation which most likely helped keep her cancer-free for this long. Joan's family knew using medical marijuana could bring back some form of control to her because she had no viable control over the cancer itself. Of course, they did find it surprising that she actually considered medical marijuana because she was such a rule-follower and the drug had been illegal for most of her life. In fact, Dawn reminisced that a few years earlier Mom point-blank asked her (in a rather harsh judgmental tone) if she had ever used marijuana. The memory brought a question to mind: *how long had Mom been considering this particular drug?*

Being a school night for Dawn, who taught, and John who just began his sophomore year in high school, meant they needed to make it home to prepare for the next day. To bring everyone together before leaving for the evening, all six of them sang "Kumbaya my Lord" while holding hands in a circle. Both Elaine and John started smiling again. Everyone exchanged hugs and kisses.

While leaving the hospital, Dawn asked her kids to compare their view of Grandma before and after they saw her. They said they didn't see much difference in her. Dawn recapped with "Yes, she has cancer. No, it's not going away. But there is good time to spend with Grandma just like it was before we became aware the cancer returned." The calendar showed September and outside the leaves hung green on their trees, but change had already started.

***

Mom considered herself a ducks-in-a-row type with everything thought out carefully and ahead of time, not last minute. She prepared to return to her independent living unit at Smith Crossing a couple of days later. Dawn waited with her in the hospital room for discharge papers to be complete and transport to arrive. The nurses entered periodically to check on Joan. With every new face she would inform the nurse, "I'm getting medical marijuana."

One nurse told her, "Good for you!" and high-fived Mom. Dawn only smiled slightly because she didn't want her mom to think she was laughing at her. Inside she was chuckling at Mom's behavior and wondering when her mom became so comfortable with announcing drug use. She had to admit she was enjoying Mom's lightened mood.

During Mom's first couple of weeks back at her unit, transitions to and from her wheelchair had become extremely difficult. Dawn remained hopeful it was a temporary setback from not having to transfer alone at the hospital and that practice would improve her ease of transitioning. Hospice saw her difficulty as a safety issue and did not want her transitioning, to and from the toilet specifically, without help. This led to Mom having to call for help and help taking too long to arrive. Mom's mood started to decline because she was losing her control.

Sharon, Lon, and Dawn wanted to keep their Mom in

independent living as long as possible because they knew a move would not positively impact her mood and would lead more quickly to death, so in a ducks-in-a-row type move, they added more care from hospice, but it was not 24/7 care.

"Elaine, would you be willing to stay with Grandma? You would still be able to attend your classes and appointments as usual."

"Sure." And so began Elaine's care-giving career.

However, a week and a half into her time, Dawn noticed Elaine looking haggard. "Talk to me. What's happening?"

Through tears, Elaine replied, "I'm not getting any sleep. Grandma needs help in the middle of the night to use the washroom, most times more than once." Dawn knew how much strength it took to help toilet Mom and how much Elaine needed sleep to function; it reminded her of when she nursed John and suffered severe sleep deprivation- not easy times.

This led to the sibling ducks-in-a-row think-tank being called together that day. Dawn contacted Visiting Angels and set up a consultation for that evening. As the director discussed the program, Dawn felt as if it were the perfect fit. A major benefit of the care included flexibility in requesting time which could be added or reduced as needed, and if Mom did not want to continue the care, all that was required was a bit more than 24-hours' notice. She was excited to have the care team start as soon as possible, that is, until Mom spoke.

"I'm not signing anything!" she said firmly.

"Mom, you need more care than the hospice team can provide, and if you decide you do not want to continue with them, there is no long-term contract. You just let them know."

Angrily she retorted with the attitude of a teenager, "No, I am not signing." And with that, the director politely wished Joan well and left.

"Mom, you're fighting me, and I'm trying to help you. Hospice is struggling to find people to cover overnight."

"Why can't Elaine stay with me?" her softer voice questioned.

"She wants to, but she isn't getting enough sleep."

"Well, I'm meeting with Smith Crossing to see about other options. I am not signing anything until then." The conversation ended, but Dawn's stress level skyrocketed. Mom's ducks-in-a-row conflicted with Dawn's ducks-in-a-row, and Dawn returned home frustrated.

Different care-givers came in and out of her unit. One day while Dawn visited, Mom told her that she called and called for help but the person did not help her. This option quickly unraveled.

Mom chose to move to the assisted living side of the complex. This gave the family two weeks to move her. While Sharon and Lon made plans to travel down from Wisconsin, Dawn, Elaine and John, worked on packing up the unit a little at a time. Dawn kept encouraging Mom to go through her closets full of clothes to pick out the ones she wanted to take, but Mom had plans to eat or play cards or she was too tired.

This move took a toll on all the kids. For Sharon and Lon, it was a little over a two-hour trip each way. For Dawn, cognitive overload affected her at work. Because these siblings always worked well as a team, they completed the job by the deadline and Mom moved to her new (and much smaller) assisted living unit as the autumnal leaves started to change color.

***

Sharon had worked on the medical marijuana paperwork just after Mom left the hospital. Dawn had received her care-giver card in the mail, but because Mom had moved rooms, she had to reapply because that mailing could not be forwarded. Dawn showed her mom the website of the dispensary and asked what she would like ordered. "Oh, I don't know; whatever you think," said her mom. Dawn's thoughts screamed in her head: *what I think... I never thought I would have a medical marijuana card and how am I supposed to know the best kind to order you?* Dawn decided to wait awhile (even thought this prevented her from keeping her ducks-in-a-row) and ask Mom again another time.

As family expected, the change to assisted living affected Mom's mood negatively and her lapses in memory became more noticeable. The woman who just a month ago played bridge weekly and was asked to play pinochle often, stopped playing. What were once thought to be hearing issues now seemed more like memory issues. Even her first passion, reading, rarely happened. This was the new "normal."

Dawn dealt with her mom's decline by spending time with her confidant, Chris. He listened to all the drama and truly held space for her. He did not judge; he did not attempt to fix the situation. If she asked for his thoughts, he considerately offered them. With his compassion and hugs- many, many hugs- Dawn managed to keep her life together. One of the sayings she offered to friends during times of struggle: you can't be there for others if you do not take care of yourself. Spending time with Chris, helped recharge her batteries to be there for her mom and her kids.

On October 26th, Mom celebrated her 88th birthday with Sharon's family in the afternoon, Dawn's family in the evening and Lon's family visited later that weekend. Spreading out the visits was the best way to keep Mom's spirits up, not to mention her unit was so small that not even half the family could fit in it. Her birthday brought to mind that this was probably the first of many lasts, as outside the window, multi-colored leaves fell gently to the ground.

With Thanksgiving quickly approaching, Dawn kept the ducks-in-a-row by making reservations at Buca di Beppo for 25 people. Another errand involved visiting the dispensary in hopes of finding something to lift Mom's mood.

When Dawn arrived at the dispensary, she rang the bell, stated her business, and like a prison, entered when the staff buzzed her in. The man who helped her was most likely half her age. He sounded knowledgeable offering information about the types of cannabis and their forms. He also took the time to discuss which of all the many kinds may be most helpful to Mom and tips on how to administer to first-time users. Dawn left with THC-infused gummies, something she never imagined doing three months prior.

A couple of hours before the reservation time at Buca di Beppo, Dawn, Elaine and John arrived at Mom's place. While the kids watched TV, Dawn talked with her mom in the next room. "Here are the gummies. The guy suggested starting with ¼ of a gummy."

"Okay, you can just put those away."

Incredulously, Dawn blurted, "Mom, today is a good day to try them. We'll be with you all day so we'll be able to see its effect, if any, on you."

"You're certainly determined, aren't you?"

Dawn paused. *I'm determined? I'M DETERMINED? You're the one who was telling everyone at the hospital you wanted medical marijuana. I was the one who never thought I'd be buying marijuana.* After she threw this mental hissy fit, out of her mouth came a calm, "Mom, I'm trying to help. You wanted me to buy this, and I want to be around you, especially the first time. You're only taking a quarter of one dose." Dawn felt like a drug-pusher.

"Fine, fine, fine." Her mother acquiesced, and they joined the kids in the other room.

Even with the reservation, there was a wait at the restaurant and Joan's family took up most of the waiting area. Mom seemed in a relatively happy mood which could have been because almost all of her family members surrounded her. In retrospect, Dawn considered her mom's claustrophobic tendencies and decided the marijuana may have actually been helping since she was not showing any discomfort with the very close quarters. Sharon and Lon both asked if she had taken the marijuana because they both felt she seemed unusually chipper.

In December, Dawn received a call from Elaine who was visiting Grandma Joan. "Grandma says she doesn't want the gummies at her place anymore." She felt some ominous "they" were going to find them, and she would be in trouble for having them.

When Dawn visited her mom, she tried to reassure her by taking out her medical cannabis card and reminding her, "See, you can legally use gummies. They are medicine for you."

"No, I don't want them here. *They* may find them." And so the darkness of Mom's paranoia began, mirroring the season's shortening span of daylight.

Throughout the winter months, Joan's struggles with memory, paranoia, and depression increased. The new normal became her having a good day where she talked, sat in her wheelchair, and took meals in the dining room. The not-so-good days included not getting out of bed, replacing talking with staring and pointing to communicate, and refusing to eat. The new normal was as unpredictable as Chicago's weather; you didn't know what

11

you were going to get, and you prepared yourself for, as well as dealt with, whatever ended up happening.

After Joan spoke with a retired Unitarian Universalist minister, Dawn called him to discuss Mom. "Your mother is ready."

"I know. I think she knew she was ready since August. I'm not trying to prolong her suffering."

The minister offered, "One of the kindest gifts is to tell her what you appreciate about her."

Dawn took these words seriously and considered what she would tell her mom next time she visited. "Mom, all those years you read the classics to me. Thank you. It is one of the most important gifts you gave me- not just passing along the love of reading but your love, of reading to me. Because of you, I read to Elaine and John. You know how much they love to read! If they have kids, I have a feeling they will pass the love of reading to them too." Dawn could not tell if her mom completely understood what she was saying, but she thought there was a softening in her eyes- perhaps of gratefulness. She continued, "So in honor of what you gave me as a child, I am going to read your favorite book, *Jane Eyre*, to you each time I visit. '*Jane Eyre* by Charlotte Bronte, Chapter 1. There was no possibility of taking a walk that day. We had been wandering....'" And thus, began how Dawn and her mom spent the rest of their time together.

During Dawn's spring break, the weather turned a little nicer (compared to the winter weather they had experienced) and she wanted to take her mom out for a stroll around the pond. As

Mom traveled from assisted living through independent-living in her electric wheelchair, people who she used to see daily greeted her with happy faces, and they briefly chatted. When Dawn and her mom finally made it to the other side of the complex and out the door, the breeze blew briskly, but the sun helped counter the chill. "It's cold out here," Mom complained.

"Let's move out into the sun. We'll go around the pond once, and go right back inside." Dawn moved quickly forward to prevent her mother from refusing the idea. With Joan's electric wheelchair at full speed they finished a revolution around the pond in no time. "Do you want to go around again?"

Mom gave a resounding, "No!" So they returned to her assisted living unit.

When Dawn returned to work the next Monday, the weather turned cooler and cloudier a.k.a. more depressing. She saw she missed some phone calls from an unknown number and Sharon. Listening to the voicemail her eyes opened wide in surprise.

"Hi, this is Debra, one of the nurses with your mom. Please call me at your earliest convenience."

"Hey, Dawn. It's your sister. Ah, Mom left the building in her wheelchair and the staff chased after her yelling for her to stop. Now either she couldn't hear them or she didn't care to do what they said. They caught up with her and coaxed her back in the building. She is okay, but they said they need to take her electric wheelchair away from her."

As her daughter and a devout rooter for the underdog, Dawn smiled at the picture of her mom "breaking away." It reminded her of when she rooted for R.P. and the Chief as they tried to escape in *One Flew Over the Cuckoo's Nest*. Of course, she knew taking away the wheelchair would not help Mom's sense of control. She also wondered if the stroll on which she took Mom the week prior had anything to do with this attempted escape. Perhaps she was experiencing her own form of spring fever.

Without her mobility, Mom's loss of will quickly showed. She only demonstrated will in refusing to help the nurses transition her, take her medicine, and go to the dining room to eat meals. These refusals would lead her to end up in skilled-nursing.

Sharon and Bruce met with assisted living administrators to discuss Mom moving to skilled-nursing. No family member was in favor of that. They had all experienced their dad's move to skilled-nursing. Within the first four months he had moved from the top quarter of functioning patients to the lowest quarter, so they fought hard to keep Mom in assisted living.

In order to manage this feat, the siblings decided to use Best Loving Care at Home, a 24/7 care provider, at her assisted living facility. At first, Mom's mood improved, but soon she returned to experiencing more bad days than good ones. The siblings concluded that much of the bad-day syndrome was the result of untreated depression. Mom refused the antidepressants, so Dawn spoke with hospice about alternatives to pills.

ABH cream (Ativan®, Benadryl®, Haldol®), when rubbed on

Joan's forearms, helped with the anxiety and agitation. It worked well. She was more tired but much less agitated.

Life was looking more positive: the extra 24/7 women provided excellent care, the ABH cream helped calm Joan, and she started the antidepressant. That is, until Joan stopped taking the antidepressant.

On Easter Sunday, after Joan's family and friends ate supper, Mom refused to eat. She decided she wanted to go to bed instead of visiting with anyone. Family would take turns entering her bedroom and talking to her. After most returned home, Mom fell asleep. Dawn and Chris talked in the living room, keeping an ear out for Mom. Dawn heard her mom move about and immediately rushed to her bedside. "Do you want to get up now?" Mom said nothing but kept moving toward the side of the bed where her wheelchair sat. "Okay, Mom, I need to call a CNA to help you transition." She just kept scooching toward the wheelchair. Dawn pressed the call button, but Mom was not waiting. "Mom, stop! We need to wait for help because I cannot do this by myself." But there was no stopping her, so Dawn decided she needed to do her best to keep her mom from falling. That's pretty much all she ended up doing.

Even though Mom had lost an incredible amount of weight since August, she could not hold up what was left on just one leg. So together, Mom and Dawn looked as if they were being shot in slow motion all. The. Way. Down. To. The. Floor. Still there was no CNA available to help. Dawn kept Mom's head from hitting the floor, but she couldn't even help Mom sit up. Neither had enough strength.

Fed up with the lack of assisted living help, Dawn called out, "Chris, please help!" Together they managed to move Mom into her wheelchair. Moments later someone from the facility finally arrived. Dawn now understood why family needed to be active participants when a loved one is in a nursing-home situation. She spoke pointedly at the employee, "I know I am not supposed to help her transition, but I buzzed a *long* time ago and she was going to fall if I didn't do something."

"Oh, I'm just here to bring Joan her dinner," the young woman said ever so meekly.

Dawn held in the rest of her anger. She would deal with it through journaling and therapy. Complaining to the director of the facility was a catch-22; if she brought it up, it would give administration another reason to move her mom to skilled-nursing and that would have a negative effect on her mom.

Within one week, Joan had fallen out of bed twice. The 24/7 care now had to be right next to her bed constantly. If they needed to use the washroom, they contacted a CNA to watch her because she would try to make another escape every time she thought she wasn't being watched.

Dawn's confidant, journaling, and regular therapy did not completely help her balance what she experienced with her mom. As much as she felt she was dealing with her mom's "new normals," she began developing cluster cold-sores. She asked herself why. *I*

16

don't feel I am disregarding my feelings, and I am not keeping *everything inside. What am I not acknowledging?* To attempt to curb the cold-sore outbreak, she turned to her creative side and made a meme:

Coincidence or not, after Dawn created the meme, she encountered no new cold sores.

Joan returned to refusing to eat, but she added a new trick. In the dining room she would begin dropping silverware, plates, and glasses- intentionally. Dawn finally said to her sister, "Mom needs to stop eating downstairs; it obviously isn't working." And so the dining room trips were no more. Of course, that meant their mom was one step closer to being forced out of assisted living.

The day administration determined Joan could no longer stay in assisted living because her needs were too great for their level of care, sadness prevailed. Hospice said she could still continue living for months according to her vitals, but 24/7 care felt she was nearing end-of-life. Dawn decided the best way to figure out when Mom was truly close was to track her vitals. If her oxygen level fell below 90, if she had a spike in temperature, if her blood pressure continued to lower, these signs showed impending death. While in some respects, death appeared to be drawing nigh, the buds on the tree branches as well as Mom's behavior during her transition contradicted this.

On a warm, sunny Thursday in May, Mom moved to skilled-nursing. 24/7 care was with her for the move and Dawn and John arrived right after school to visit. Dawn coaxed Mom into her wheelchair, and John pushed his grandmother around the area. As they traveled through skilled-nursing and memory care, Mom would point to where she wanted to go. She did not speak, but they were pleased that she was actively participating. When they reached the doorway out of skilled-nursing, John began turning the wheelchair to the right to continue the circle around the area. Grandma adamantly held her hand up to stop and pointed back toward the door. Dawn enthusiastically suggested, "Let's see what's this way, Mom!" and John continued the circular trip back to her room. Mom's arm collapsed into her lap, she shrugged her shoulders and shook her head in disapproval. Her drivers were preventing her escape.

When they made it back to her room, she kept pointing to continue the trip, so she and John did just that while Dawn returned to assisted living to pick up pictures to personalize Mom's new room.

The next day Dawn brought Elaine to see Grandma. "Hi, Grandma," Elaine smiled as she spoke. Turning to Dawn, she asked, "Was she like this yesterday?"

"Well..."

She sounded distraught, "I missed seeing her being

interactive?"

"It is hit or miss, Elaine. Talking to her and holding her hand are still things she likes, even if she doesn't acknowledge them the way she used to." Elaine spent time with Grandma while Dawn read aloud more of *Jane Eyre* neither knowing how much she would understand, but both knowing they were there for her.

On Sunday Sharon, Lon, and Bruce visited Mom. Dawn joined them later that day. They talked with each other, and they each talked to Mom while they held her hand. All knew Mom wasn't eating and drinking enough to sustain life, but no one knew how long she would live.

Monday rolled around, and after work Dawn read to Mom who was less responsive each day. Another new normal. Dawn knew she could not change it; all she had control of was reading her mom's favorite book.

Tuesday, Sharon left a voicemail for Dawn who was at work. At lunchtime, she returned the call. "Hi, Sharon. What's up?"

"Hospice says Mom is actively dying. They will be providing a 24-hour caregiver for her starting tonight at 9:30."

"Okay. What were her vitals? Did she spike a temperature?"

"No, no temperature. Her blood pressure was a little lower and her oxygenation level was right on the borderline."

"I was heading over after work; I'll make sure I leave as soon as possible." All Dawn could think was that Geneva, the 24/7 care provider, would only be there until 2 p.m. and the soonest she could make it was 3:30. She did not want her mom to die alone.

Dawn arrived before 3:30, noticing her mom's breathing immediately. The deep, heavy inhales reminded her of her dad's breathing hours before he passed, but there wasn't as long a pause between them for her.

"Hi, Mom. It's Dawn," she greeted her while touching her hand. Mom moved her hand away, as if the touch hurt her. Soon after, her Mom's nurse entered and Dawn requested, "Please tell me her latest vitals."

"Let me take them again right now." She placed the oximeter on Joan's finger and then fitted the blood pressure cuff on her arm and inflated it. Dawn watched as the needle descended and waited for the numbers. "I'm going to try that again." After the second attempt, Dawn realized the nurse could not obtain a reading. The oximeter read 88 which was lower than the morning reading. "I'll be back at six for her ABH treatment. Is there anything you need?"

Dawn shook her head and turned toward the windowsill where she noticed the tree branches with their buds. She grabbed *Jane Eyre*, pulled up a chair, and covered her mom's hand with the sheet. When Dawn placed her hand on top, her mom did not flinch, so she began reading.

During the chapter, her mom became agitated. "Mom, they'll be able to give you your medicine..." Dawn looked at her phone which read 5:15 and thought *I can't say soon. Forty-five minutes is not soon!* As she ran her fingers through her mom's hair to soothe her, she realized it was not helping.

Dawn returned to reading in hopes of her voice being more calming than her touch was managing. Every now and again she looked at her mom who eventually relaxed. About the third time she looked up after that point, she paused her reading. *Quiet- too quiet.* Dawn studied her mom's chest and didn't see movement. She moved away the sheet and placed her hand over her mom's. No flinching. She pressed the call button and waited. And waited. And waited. She called the nurses' station with her cell phone but no one answered.

Since no one was responding and Dawn did not want to leave the room, she called hospice and heard the voicemail pick up. *You've got to be kidding me. I can't get a hold of anyone?* "This is Dawn Plestina. I cannot reach the nurse directly, and I do not think my mom is breathing." As she ended the call, the nurse arrived.

The nurse examined Joan, and then looked sympathetically at Dawn, who waited to hear what the nurse found. When no words were forthcoming she asked, "Did she pass?" Dawn never heard the nurse answer.

Suddenly, hospice entered and examined Joan. Again, no definitive words. Dawn felt frustrated and wondered if they were worried she would break down. All Dawn wanted was the determination of the vitals from the professionals. She then placed her hand on her mom's again- this time she felt cool to the touch. Dawn now knew.

21

Hospice then softly spoke, "Is there anyone you want to notify before they take Mom?"

"Yes, Elaine and John will want to see her."

***

Joan's memorial service happened just as she planned it years ago (her final set of ducks-in-a-row.) Her friend from the Unitarian Universalist Church officiated; Chris played "Turn! Turn! Turn!" on acoustic guitar while his band mate sang; and Sharon, Lon, and Dawn eulogized their mother.

Dawn included in her eulogy, this excerpt from *Jane Eyre* which she found particularly meaningful:

"I came to see you, Helen; I heard you were very ill, and I could not sleep till I had spoken to you."

"You came to bid me good-bye, then; you are just in time probably."

"Are you going somewhere, Helen? Are you going home?"

"Yes; to my long home—my last home."

"But where are you going to, Helen? Can you see? Do you know?"

"I believe; I have faith; I am going to God."

"Where is God? What is God?"

"My Maker and yours, who will never destroy what he created. I rely implicitly on his power, and confide wholly in

---

> *his goodness: I count the hours till that eventful one arrives which shall restore me to him, reveal him to me."*
>
> *"You are sure, then, Helen, that there is such a place as heaven; and that our souls can get to it when we die?"*
>
> *"I am sure there is a future state; I believe God is good; I can resign my immortal part to him without any misgiving. God is my father; God is my friend; I love him; I believe he loves me."*
>
> *"And shall I see you again, Helen, when I die?"*
>
> *"You will come to the same region of happiness; be received by the same mighty, universal Parent, no doubt, dear Jane."*

Just as Jane remained with Helen as she died, Dawn felt thankful that she remained by her mom's side, reading her favorite book as her mom died. While many people think of cold and darkness when they consider death, Dawn felt her mom's passing on a sunny day in the springtime suited her finale more appropriately. Her mom was no longer hindered physically or mentally or emotionally; she escaped these impediments.

She *is* free.

My Winter Morning Coffee and Cigarette

by Kenn Kimpell

The rising whispers of rubber tires rubbing streets
are heard as their blurs and disappear.
Chilled breezes sift these barren trees and I echo
a selfish breath: inhale... exhale.
The billowing smoke is a prism for the rising light.

My mug steams, alerting my focus
to where acidic aromas of vanilla await.
I'm being seduced by this allure I lust.
I warm my mouth and burn my tongue
dropping the cold handle of this hot ceramic.

For Lack of a Name...

I died.

We are all rivers, and ourselves are water, and I've long since flowed.

The kid you grew up with—the one on the bus, the playground, next door,

in the classroom, at his desk, in the hallway, in detention, at home,

the kid who held Luke (not Han Solo, never Vader) as his hero,

the kid who thrice crushed on you,

but you didn't know,

or you did but it wasn't reciprocated,

or it was but he was too afraid to say so,

the kid who met you as a prepubescent,

with shards of shell still speckled on his coat,

with childhood dreams still within his notebook,

who then strove to be a poet,

but who repressed that poem

tossed to some never-ever-after,

who then never ever tried again,

with whom you partied and smoked, and whom you got drunk with,

with whom you formed a band, sang Nirvana, and whom you broke up with,

with whom you worked and laughed, and whom you had lived with,

with whom you danced and then made-out, and whom you had slept with,

with you, who discovered spoken-word, only to never—not once—speak to again,

who, through you, only realized too late her forewarnings of 'cynicism and defeat',

whose never-ending song sang softer—diminished and minor—ever after,

whose tones lamented that 'heartbreak', this 'hatred', his 'war',

whose dreams decayed to Lovecraftian terror,

anxiety, and nightmares,

and yet, who'd still prefer to remain asleep;

that kid, the teen, the adult, that man,

the brother, the cousin, the son, that friend,

the coworker, the boss, the student, your lover—Kenn,

is dead.

—A. Name

Times and Seasons in This Place

by Paula Morris Thomas

I'm so thankful for THIS PLACE during this season of my life.

As I sat in the quiet of my living room, listening to the motor's hum from the box fan that lightly blew on me, regulating body heat and furnace heat causing them to exist in a happy marriage, I entertained thoughts of how so very busy, disjointed, packed with last minute demands and an overwhelming "to do" list my life evolved into during 2018…and is still ongoing through September 2019. And as I mentally listed the things in my life that put the capital "W" in the word "work" I reflected on one of the few "works" that's actually a labor of love. It's the time I spend at the New Lenox Library (in New Lenox, Illinois) with my literary family.

I miss being in THIS PLACE when I'm unable to attend our scheduled meetings due to one of the "million" reasons that seem to show up in my life lately. And most of the time, during this season when I do show up, I'm running on fumes because the life I've been living has zapped me of most my strength. The saving grace is in getting to THIS PLACE.

It's in THIS PLACE that I'm able to divorce myself from the weight of the world for 90 minutes…(well, 105 minutes if I get here on time)…[wink, wink, Jim].

It's in THIS PLACE, whether I bring some written piece to share, or just lend voice to what's shared by one of our literary family members, that I'm able to exercise a precious gift that's been eluding me lately. The gift of exhale, relax, just let life unfold.

In THIS PLACE it's not that I don't make any mistakes in my writing, but that my literary family recognizes that I write from my heart and they're willing to hear what my heart has to say. Their critiques are gentle and designed to enhance the truth of who I am...and propel me into the deepest realm my soul's pen can write from.

Outside of THIS PLACE I'm still asked how many other Black people are part of the group. In THIS PLACE I don't feel obligated to represent the Black population in America...and yet if there's a topic that I can bring insight and clarity to, I'm willing, ready and able...but not obligated. Because in THIS PLACE I'm not relegated as the only Black member in the group. I'm simply a member and fellow writer who's learning to be a better writer and orator with the help of some amazing people.

In THIS PLACE I am proud to call the people I have met both family and friend.

This is my haven...and I hope that we'll have many more seasons of fellowship, fun and "flirting" with the gift of writing...IN THIS PLACE.

Seasonally yours,
Paula Morris Thomas

There Were Many Rainy Days

by Diane Perry

How do I begin this story? Let me go back to high school. When I was a junior, I did not know which career path to choose once I graduated. It was like the game of "Life," which route do I choose? Should I start work immediately or attend college for four years? I was leaning toward college since my three older sisters attended and landed in fine careers. So once my decision was made, I did not know which major to choose.

One day, while riding on the school bus, I overheard conversations. One girl said she wanted to become a cop, another said she wanted to start classes leaning towards nursing. Confused about what my choice was, my friend, Darlene, suggested to me, "Why don't you try Journalism? You like writing."

I agreed with her, and my next year, senior year, I enrolled in a Journalism course. My teacher, Mrs. Owatta, wanted her class to participate with the student newspaper. She posted many positions for the paper starting from Editor-in-Chief, to News Editor to Sports Editor. I applied for two positions. After our writing samples were reviewed, she assigned me as the Sports Editor. I was excited that she chose me, and especially for sports. In addition to this, we were all challenged to write for any news beat. I mainly wrote on sports, attending many basketball games or swim meets, but also wrote feature stories on some of our best athletes. Being voted the quietest girl of my senior class of 500 students, I felt compelled to work on my social skills. Being a newspaper reporter helped me to overcome my shyness. Upon filling out applications my last semester of high school, I was accepted to attend Eastern Illinois University in the fall, intriguing me with their excellent journalism program.

As my first semester started at the university, I chose many general education courses including Algebra, English and Sociology. My only journalism class was "Intro to Journalism 101." After a few weeks in the class, Dr. Voltz referred to the syllabus, stating we were required to present an oral report about the media. After hearing this, and not being able to sleep at night, I dropped the class because I realized I was too shy to read in front of a group of people. Public speaking was not an easy task for me. Furthermore, I thought this was going to be a writing course.

My second semester, I enrolled in some business courses, thinking the business world might be an area of interest for me. After attending an Economics course for a whole semester suffering through all the concepts of "supply and demand," I nearly failed the course, which led me to think about another area of interest. During this year, I switched my major from Psychology, to Community Health, and finally back to Journalism which seemed to be the match for me. I loved writing and composing.

I was encouraged by another Journalism student to write for the Daily Eastern News because upon graduation a portfolio was a necessity for a job interview. Immediately, I started working for them composing many headings for articles, and writing stories.

One of my articles I remember to this day was about "Coors Beer" expanding from the Rocky Mountains of Colorado to Illinois (1983). I called long distance from the newspaper office to interview a polite man from the Coors Brewing Company. My article was published the next week with my byline, "Diane Nowak." Not only did I write for the newspaper, but for the Eastern Alumnus, a university magazine as well.

Since I changed my major three times, I needed to attend college for an extra semester. After four and a half years of finishing the required curriculum, I graduated with my B.A. in Journalism. As I walked through the procession with my black cap and gown, beaming with confidence, I was convinced my working years would be "easy picking." After all, this was the best day for the rest of my life since I had the piece of paper.

Returning to the Chicagoland area in January, I started interviewing for newspaper writing positions. I received a monthly journalism job posting newsletter from Eastern, as well as corresponding with my academic counselor, Dr. Mary Wohlrabe. She encouraged me to continue with my studies in Journalism while attending college since my parents continually discouraged me.

I found one posting and interviewed for a stringer/reporter position for the Hammond Times, and was hired. My dad drove me all the way from Posen to Hammond, Indiana to get my weekly assignments, and to interview my sources either in Illinois or Indiana. It was quite overwhelming and hectic for me as I ended up in tears. Dad was very supportive of my achievements, but said to me on many occasions, "Why don't you quit that journalism?"

Consequently, Dad said I could live at home as long as I needed because he saw I was struggling. At this time, I was twenty-three years old and my cousin, Moe, being twenty, obtained a successful career as a managerial secretary in a bank. She was engaged to be married. My dad and mom were not supportive of journalism because it was not lucrative. I was paid by the inch of the story and not a salary. I know they wanted more for me.

Dad said, "Why don't you go to that Fox Secretarial College like Moe did and become a secretary? She got the best deal; she has a job and is getting married."

At this time, I was not thinking of marriage at all. When I was in college with my studies, I was inspired by a woman war correspondent. In my eyes, she encouraged my love for Journalism. I wrote a paper expressing my interest as a news correspond and did not want to commit myself to marriage until I was at least twenty-six years old. I wanted a career first.

Meanwhile, my position at the Hammond Times did not last more than two months and I quit. I wrote to Dr. Wohlrabe about my decision to get a position as a secretary in a company as my parents wanted. She wrote back saying, "Diane, you struggled with your decision to graduate with your Bachelors in Journalism, obtained a job as a writer and now you are quitting? Why?" She knew about all the flack my parents gave me while attending college. After this letter, I never heard from her again.

In the spring, I started a full-time receptionist/secretarial position for a construction and development company on Ontario Street, Chicago. My salary was $12,000. My journalism efforts were still utilized as a part-time freelance writer for The Star newspaper in Chicago Heights. I worked there for five years. I had three front-page articles.

As time went on, life happens, meaning my sister got married and five months later, my dad passed away. I quit the construction company and was hired as a proofreader for an accounting firm. After the tax season, I was laid off and was devastated because there were not too many jobs out there. The job market was turbulent.

My mother said criticizingly, "Diane, if you are such a great writer, someone would have hired you by now. You need to do something else. Go to Fox Secretarial College." She added, "I will make your first payment."

I wasn't sure if Mom just hated journalism or wanted to upset me sometimes with her hurtful comments. I remember one time when she and Dad got in an argument, she ripped up Dad's garden picture of him that I developed in my Photojournalism class. At the time I cried and Dad sympathetically said, "I don't know why she does things like that."

Mom and I made our visit to Fox College. As I registered, she willingly wrote out the first check for my tuition. There were quarterly payments and I would complete their program of one year including typing, shorthand, and accounting courses. One year later, my savings account was drained and I was ready to start working. They had a career placement center and the college president, Mr. K, had many employment contacts.

Once I graduated with my certification, I interviewed with an advertising firm thinking possibly this would be a stepping stone to my writing career, but it wasn't. It was a boring position so I asked Fox College to place me again and they did. The next job was at First Chicago where my cousin, Moe, (now divorced) worked. This job was definitely busier but it wasn't quite what I wanted. I worked as a secretary for salespeople in the Letters of Credit department. It was time for me to move on. Not only was it unsatisfying, but it was not enough money to support myself. At this time, most of my friends (game of Life again) were either married or made a decent salary to afford an apartment. My goal was to keep looking through the classified job ads.

Diligently looking, I saw an ad for a secretarial position to the Building Manager of the Chicago Tribune tower. I interviewed and was offered the position. My salary boosted to $20,000 a year. Working at the Tribune, I already knew there was no way for me to wiggle over to newspaper side to become a writer. Although Journalism was still in my heart, I was happy I could move on with my life.

By July of this year, I found an apartment with the cheapest rent including heat. It was on the second floor of a four-dwelling building in Brookfield. By the time I paid my rent, car note and my monthly train fare for my job downtown, I only had $28.00 left for two weeks. I managed, but it was tough. I bought cheap protein like hot dogs, ground beef and eggs. Mom supplied me with some canned vegetables from her pantry. I hardly went out because it would be using gas and I never ate out unless Mom treated me. My position at the Tribune lasted two years until I decided to look for another career. I always complained because I couldn't buy anything extra for myself. My clothes were getting outdated.

One day, Mom and I were sitting on her front porch and she gave me a letter from Metropolitan Life which was inserted with her premium bill. It was an opportunity to become a sales representative.

After reading the letter, I said smiling to Mom convincingly, "A lot of my friends are salespeople and they make $45,000 a year. Maybe I should try it. I have a lot of stamina for working."

She agreed nodding, "Check into it."

I interviewed with a manager at Metropolitan Life in Frankfort. He said I needed to first get licensed in "Property and Casualty" and "Life and Health" to sell insurance. After purchasing the books, and attending night classes, I took the state exams obtaining the licensure for both. I sent out a lot of letters with the MetLife logo on them to possible clients and made cold calls to set up appointments. I started selling insurance for MetLife in 1990 and continued for two years. I almost lost everything I owned because I could not make the quota. Selling insurance is difficult because it is an intangible item, it's not like selling vacuum cleaners. I cried myself to sleep at night because I had to use my savings account to pay my expenses. Maybe a secretarial job wasn't so bad? At least it is a steady income every two weeks.

My mother often said after this happening, "I'm so sorry I gave you that damn letter."

Immediately, I quit sales and went back to secretarial work. I did not want to be complacent in any job because I wasn't being challenged, in conclusion; not making enough money to live on. I routinely switched jobs every two years because the raises weren't enough nor were there any opportunities for overtime pay. My desire to go back to school wasn't practical because I worked in the city. There was no online schooling like there is now. I finally got the chance to get back in school when I worked near a community college one year later. However, I needed to work retail as well. It was difficult to work two jobs, attend classes twice a week, and have quality time to study. I tried it but my concentration was not clear when taking exams. My plan was to complete Biology, then Human Anatomy and Physiology before applying to a Nursing program, however; my grades weren't good enough.

By this time in my life, I was thirty-two. I attended my cousin, Janice's wedding who was thirty-one and younger than me. I still didn't have my life together. Sure, I wanted to be married and have children but there was no one I was dating nor anyone who would want me. I felt insecure about myself. I remember the saying, "first you have to complete yourself before you can find your mate."

One Sunday, I attended a church picnic and saw a young couple with a baby. I cried because I thought, I will probably never get the chance to have a baby. My life was not going as I planned.

My friend Donna and I had a conversation over dinner one night. She was a legal secretary in a small law firm. "Why don't you work for attorneys? I make a good salary. I demand a raise if he doesn't give me one. Since I got divorced, I have to support my daughter."

Desperately, as I listened, I said, "I will look into it."

I went to an employment agency. The lady said, "You have to type at least 80 to 90 words per minute to qualify for a large law firm like Kirkland and Ellis or Katten, Muchin & Zavis. Your typing speed is only 65 words per minute. Also, they want experience from a large law firm to work there. With your computer skills I can line up an interview with Aon Corporation's law department."

I interviewed at Aon and got hired. I worked for this company for two years and they moved. I obtained another job for bankruptcy attorneys. After two years, they moved. These thunderstorms of rain and cloudy grey skies continued until a rainbow showed me the way. Finally, I went to school to get a license to work as a Certified Nursing Assistant as I worked two jobs. I was hired as a nursing assistant for the night shift, and started to attend classes one semester at a time to get the general curriculum for nursing. My grades were outstanding as I studied for one class at a time. I applied for the Nursing and the Respiratory Therapy program. I was accepted to Respiratory and graduated with an Associate's Degree. I have worked in this career for the last eight years being challenged and financially satisfied.

Today, I'm 56 and look back at all my financial struggles. I felt like I was just spinning my wheels for twenty years through the mud and snow keeping my nose to the grindstone to survive. I am not "seasoned" in any occupation but still trying to be great at something. Respectfully, I call myself the "Jill of all Trades." Being happily-married, we work together in a comfortable lifestyle. My husband has had the same struggles, and he understands. To anyone looking in, it all looks like sunshine. I can't stand it when someone says, "Oh, you didn't want children" or people looking at us as DINKS – meaning Double-Income and NO KIDS, money, money, money. We wanted kids but unfortunately, we weren't blessed with kids. Although it all looks sunny, we have both had our share of clouds for many years when we were single.

Seasonal Haiku

by Cora Nawracaj

SPRING

You are so alive

Bursting with many colors

And beautiful smells

SUMMER

Sometimes, you're sultry

Fry an egg on the sidewalk

I love you the best?

FALL

Soon the leaves will fall

Kaleidoscope of colors

Yes, trees shed their coats

WINTER

I see naked trees

Waiting for their coat of snow

Sparkle in the sun

All of the seasons

I was blessed to be with you

I wish there were more

What about Heaven?

Do they have seasons up there?

Peace, Love, Faith and Joy

Yes, another spring

I am thankful to be here

My seventy-first

How did this happen?

Lord, the years are flying by

Not yet, God, not yet

Want to keep going

More Joy, more laughter, less tears

To have more seasons

Yes- a "Bucket List"

So many things come to mind

"Disneyland" one last time

Seasons of Time

by Emilia Weindorfer

For everything there is a season, and a time for every purpose under heaven.

There is a time to be born and a time to die. No one knows the exact date of either one.

There is a time to plant, and a time to harvest that which is planted. A home gardener is advised to wait until May 15 to plant crops if you live in Zone 5, the Chicagoland area to guarantee that frost damage will not occur. Farmers have their own timetables to plant their crops.

There is a time to kill, and a time to heal. Wartime scenarios create justification to kill for one's country. At other times, self-defense warrants this act. People heal from the loss of a loved one, their job, their health, friendship, residence, and political candidate.

There is a time to break down, and a time to build up. Crossword puzzles and Legos are broken down into segments, then built up again into a cohesive whole. Teachers break down subject matter into understandable units.

There is a time to weep, and a time to laugh. Weeping is for loss of what is dear.

There is a time to seek and a time to lose. To seek peace, we find a safe refuge. To seek answers to facts or questions we use reference materials or go online. Sometimes seeking an answer to a problem or dilemma is often found in another person. God is often sought to achieve spiritual strength.

When we read a book that we totally love, we lose ourselves in a rapt state. We lose weight by dieting. We lose sports games in competition. We lose another person who is following us by hiding from them. We lose bets on horse races. We lose items that we need such as keys or eyeglasses.

There is a time to keep and a time to cast away. We keep useful or valuable items. This can take the form of a collection such as sports memorabilia. Someone may ask us to keep a secret. People say we are a "keeper" if we are treasured by them. We keep food cold by using refrigeration or hot with an insulated container. Discussions are kept going by knowledgeable participation. A time to cast away would be to throw a fishing line into the water. Casting away archaic ideas can be accomplished by flashes of insight or maturity. Cast away packaging after taking the merchandise out of the box. Cast away garbage for sanitary reasons. "Cast away, cast away, cast away all" is a famous saying. "Cast away your cares and woes" are beginning lyrics from the song "Bye Bye Blackbird."

There is a time to rend and a time to sow. Losing a loved one can rend the heart into distress. Dropping a glass onto a stone floor will rend it useless. A head on crash between two cars rends both a total wreck. There are timetables to sow vegetables. Gardeners are familiar with them. Some people sow rumors and dissension.

There is a time to keep silence, and a time to speak. When a teacher is presenting her lesson in class, her students maintain silence. A guest lecturer in an auditorium also commands silence. When mom is chastising her child for an infraction, the child hopefully maintains silence. When an artisan or craftsman is demonstrating how to create something, his audience maintains silence. We speak when asked for advice. We speak when answering the phone or door. We speak responses to liturgy at Mass. We speak to friends and coworkers in conversation. We speak to sales clerks in stores. We speak to the medical staff when undergoing an examination. We speak up to help keep someone out of harm's way.

There is a time to love and a time to hate. We love our parents, grandparents, husband and children. We show love to other relatives, and our neighbors. We love our jobs, gardens, a clean house, beautiful music and art work. We love our country and all the freedoms and privileges of a democracy. We love clean air and water, animals and wildlife. We love good food and drink. We love those appliances that save us work. We hate dishonesty, bigotry, selfishness, and diseases that kill us.

There is a time for war and a time for peace. War is warranted when our enemy attempts to invade our country and destroy our freedoms. Peace occurs when everything is done according to established rules. Harmony can then exist. Peace comes with kindness for all.

The seasons of life are multifaceted. We enter this world

alone, stay for a while, and place our footprint on our universe. We exit alone. We alone decide how we wish to be remembered and what contributions will be our legacy.

The Fourth Stage

by Marlene Lees

Our ladies meeting started as usual this season with everyone coming in and greeting those friends they knew. The women attending were a diverse group bridging different ages and interests. I was always remarkably surprised by the accomplishments of such seemingly simple people and amazed at the talent hidden so unexpected in those of our very own neighborhood. It was going to be an eventful meeting as the topic was to be engaging and highlighted self-improvement.

I noticed one woman who came as the guest of a friend. Among the women, she stood out because of her manner. She seemed distracted. Since I was the moderator, I wondered if she was comfortable coming to the meeting as she seemed to be so very deep in preoccupied thought. It was her first time attending, but as I watched, her manner didn't really appear to have anything to do with being new to the group.

I struggled to observe her without being noticed. There was, again, a striking difference in her as compared to the ladies who come out for a casual lunch, socializing and to listen to whatever presenter and topic is scheduled. It's a relaxed setting, nothing threatening, and yet she seemed to be apprehensive, looking as if she was preoccupied and somewhat disturbed, not perturbed. She really seemed to be concerned about something that was really troubling her.

Could something have happened to her recently? What did she have on her mind? What was she ruminating about so intently? What was upsetting her? What was overshadowing her that she couldn't get an answer to? Could it be a health issue? Could it be a recent loss? Was it some life change event? Was it something she had to do and didn't want to do?

Everyone who comes to the meeting is allocated a few minutes to introduce themselves and give a synopsis in something of interest about themselves. I wondered if she would be comfortable sharing something of herself relative to this perplexing problem.

The meeting opened and we proceeded in our normal and routine fashion. It is a welcoming setting and everyone is eager to talk and share experiences. As the meeting danced through its formalities, we started at one end of the u-shaped table to begin those confident and usually colorful, albeit heart-warming and powerful individual self-descriptions and heartfelt disclosures.

As we inched around the table, it soon became this new guest's opportunity to tell us who she was and something of herself. She stated she was a guest of her friend, they had recently met, and this was how she got the opportunity to come. It was now that I began to hold my breath, as I was so very curious as to whether we would find out even something of what was on her mind.

She then easily and quite naturally let us know how comfortable she was in our group setting as she went through her recent past experiences quickly and began to explain she wanted to tell of us a recent experience. I now couldn't wait to hear what she was about to say that had her so preoccupied in such an overly apprehensive way.

She began to explain that she had recently retired and a friend had thoughtfully described to her that she was now in the Fourth Stage of her life! She highly accented the description of Fourth Stage and delivered this information as if she is looking into her future as a dismal abyss.

I gasped inwardly. She seemed a little uneasy and as if she didn't know what she was to do next or think next or even know how to manage now in this Fourth Stage of her life. She explained this as if she had never heard five scarier words! She seemed really concerned, upset, confused, and apprehensive, as she faced this foreboding concept as presented to her. Many people find it a bit of a sudden shock when retiring. It involves facing an unfamiliar future, a new week but without a schedule.

She wasn't the only one in a confusing situation where one feels limited. There is also the student, standing at the close of a graduation ceremony with diploma in hand wondering: "what now?" There are those who feel they are looking at nothingness when a job is lost, the parents that feel the difference when the kids have just left for college. There is the patient when an illness surfaces or the soul when the death of a loved one devastates and numbs feeling.

I knew I had to offer what I could to give her a good perspective and let her see that the description of life recently given her is limiting in vision and there is so much out there to engage in. It is sad her friend made it sound as though she were looking into an ominous vista and a dreary void.

This was a theme that resonated with my understanding. My thoughts raced through an assortment of experiences. I had so many thoughts converging all at once, my heart went out to her as I wanted to share so much of what I find is a threshold to something great. I wondered if I would become tongue-tied trying to say the many things I was thinking to say all at once.

It was time to reveal, kindly, and with care that there is life after the job or career you just retired from. I began by explaining that many people find it an unexpected shock when they retire. It is because they are suddenly removed from the familiar people and places, the dutiful schedule, and have no real commitments in place initially to do much of anything.

I then went on to suggest that, in this, is a beautiful moment before you. A new opportunity to accomplish what you have always wanted to do and did not have the time to do. There may even be many things that interest you, not just one thing you never had time for. Some say, once in their new pattern of doing what they love, that they don't know how they ever had time for work!

Afore you lies the opportunity for just enjoying life. There may be the chance to include time for group activities in an assortment of settings or even volunteering. All of these choices can provide dear friendships and a real sense of belonging. Yet some people like myself go into other careers, home based businesses, authoring, and any assortment of energetic endeavors. But, at this point, she didn't seem comforted that life was not over or at least productive, fruitful or that it could have any substance or real value. So, I continued with, "It boils down to the way we look at things and the choices we make not only in what we do, but in the way we think."

The way we think has a huge impact on us. It can be so very self-defeating or so very illuminating, invigorating, exciting and interesting. It depends on us and the decisions we make about how we want to look at things. If it is perceived as limiting unto itself and self-defeating, there is an image of life perceived as foreboding. It's now about what you can do about this approaching future and the ground work you provide to let it develop.

As interests surface, so do the endless possibilities as you enter this new, unchoreographed, bare area that has no script, no set, no backdrop, no music, no audience. Let's call it a stage as your friend did, in this case, a Fourth Stage. It is quiet, lonely, empty, yet peaceful, like winter, which is a true season in life. Can you see yourself in the light of having been seasoned with life experiences, which can serve you in so many ways at this new interval?

This stage, so empty now, is just waiting to be filled with laughter, music, motion and any number of things. It is about what you want, what you like, and how you "set" the stage is up to you right now. Feel free to awaken possibilities long dormant. At the moment, you are the only performer, you are the director, the producer, the writer, the choreographer, the scene painter and designer. You are also the auditioner. It is up to you who you want to add to this stage in this play, who you want to "play" with, if you will, and even how you want to do that. It's about what you want, what you like, and it can be up to you, if you like, to set the stage, engage the participants, have fun bantering with the script even before a story begins to unfold. Can you fathom a bit of a spark of the sensational in what is to come?

As each interest surfaces, you now have time to pledge ingenuity to a series of events as they begin to stretch out before you. You may now begin to season those thoughts and interests with intention. Season them with your talents. Every new idea requires seeds be planted that eventually bloom and grow creating a new scene, a new season, a new time in your life. One that you can season with laughter and fun resulting in happiness. While you are planting these seeds, and sprinkling in time and talent, the seeds can bloom and grow into a season you did not expect.

The choices you make will bring new people into your life along with unexpected friendships and experiences as a new season is created. We know each new season is comprised of its own colors and sounds, smells and feelings. There are seasons within seasons. The hurricane season occurs during the spring season and there are many and varied seasons within our career season. As we recognize we have been seasoned with memorable intervals and with treasured moments, the stage offers a new opportunity. The opportunity includes many components to craft a new season to enjoy.

Indian-American author Deepak Chopra helps us understand how to let go of the past and the certainty that goes with it. It becomes clear that certainty exists only in the past. One can realize that things of that past no longer apply to what we are about to do. They are merely experiences, already passed. Every minute that unfolds before us is peppered with uncertainty. I truly believe if we embrace uncertainty with creativity, we empower ourselves to have faith in our future.

Getting started is all in how you look at it; Plan it. You can look back at the many seasons and stages of your life with fond memories, seeing the learning curves, the difficulties you have overcome, and more. But, to create a new season, I have to say I believe most in what Roy T. Bennett said: "Don't be pushed around by the fears in your mind. Be led by the dreams in your heart." If it's in how you look at it, if this is the Fourth Stage of your life, what are your going to do about stage five? Six? Seven? Eight and beyond?

In the Good Ole Summertime

by Diane Perry

The tulips have sprouted,

Tree blossoms bloom white,

Lilac bushes smell fragrant,

Red cherries develop to sight.

Feel the temperature climbing

Finally, kids are out of school,

The bright sun is blinding,

Inviting all to hit the pool.

The hot weather is balmy,

Everyone wearing shorts,

Drinking a Bud Light Lime,

Playing golf, or seeing a sport.

The warm breeze picks up,

Kids screaming fly a kite,

While Mom lying in a hammock,

Throws back an icy cold Sprite.

The vegetable garden has grown,

Rows of many seeds so neat,

A sliced tomato or cucumber

On a bun with grilled meat.

When camping near the lake,

Trout fishing is required,

Many biting fish caught,

Are pan-fried by campfire.

We see fireflies and June bugs,

Roasting marshmallows is fun,

Dad playing guitar and singing,

The House of the Rising Sun.

Dining at an outdoor café,

Now that we are in the city,

To walk or bike on the lakefront,

Night lights looking so pretty.

A visit to the farmer's market,

For the next day out at the beach,

Some enjoy cheese and crackers,

While others enjoy a fresh-picked peach.

Tell Me about Love...

by Carolyn Hill

When the reality of loving is better than the dream, the heart's hidden lock opens with a key of intoxicating euphoria. Sometimes, the heart must face the possibility a particular love is not meant to be. Being in love is a self-discovery into the unknown union of two people, who believe in the moment. Its fever can be magical, and what fairytales are made of. Or it can be filled with the anxiety of what we want each other to be.

Somewhere I read, "Love may be harder to find in some people, but when they do love, you know it must be something marvelous." No one seems to escape the mischievous escapades of the mythical chubby cheeked Cupid, whose golden arrow can cause a wanton heart to fall deep in love. Sometimes his arrow is leaden to ignite aversion, and two people fall apart only to realize how much they need to fall back together. My friend Cody never gave up hope on this premise even though the daily odds were mounting against him.

Cody was searching for love almost up to his untimely death. It was hard to imagine such a powerful man of the world would have fallen prey to the ploys of a bad love. I remember a deep mellow voice of calm, which seemed to comfort all those he came in contact with including me.

Today was no different. I never knew what to expect when I stepped through the doorway of his office. From the expression on his face, I could tell he was in a different place mentally. Were we contemplating mergers, or life? He pointed to the chair and as usual I sat down.

"Got a minute?" I always had a minute. That minute made me the highest paid assistant just about anywhere. It allowed me to have a dream job, and a secret world I had to keep hidden every day I walked into the office.

"Liz, I need to brainstorm on the personal, you mind?" I made myself comfortable wondering what I could possibly offer this man of the world, except to patiently listen, again.

As I waited, I remembered happy coffee breaks and lunches filled with laughter. Even during the good times, there was an air of underlying want in Cody's voice; a sort of emptiness that comes from a mourning heart. In between sips, Cody would shrug his shoulders and sigh and look at me as if I had the answer to his want.

"Liz, I can put a billion dollar deal together, but not quite hit the target when it comes to love. What am I missing here in the equation?"

"I don't think there is an equation Cody. Like one of your deals you have to want it bad enough. And sometime relationships aren't meant to be. The one thing I do know, real love is never wavering no matter how bad the roller coaster ride of emotions maybe."

"Maybe." He tilted his head down to roll up his custom oxford sleeves, smiled and leaned over the desk and grabbed my hand. His spirit seemed broken over something he couldn't shake off. That kind of something so many of us haul from one relationship to another. Little did I know his dilemma was a deliberate roadblock to his happiness and mine.

"Liz, don't you ever get tired of the game playing yourself?"

"Sure Cody."

Oh, how I understood his heartfelt emotion, for I often pondered the bitter-sweet rat-race to find that special someone over the years. It seems everyone comes with some kind of emotional baggage. The trick is to find someone to help you unpack.

Cody seemed more relaxed. He smiled, his eyes brightened, "I knew the first time I saw her, she was the one. I felt like a kid again. What about you Liz?"

"What a bummer," I thought. "Me? Well, no one in particular." All the while my heart cried out, "see me, see me."

"That's my problem," Cody mumbled. "I've known her a long time, and I don't know if she will say 'yes'" Cody let go of my hand and sat back and turned toward the window. "Look at that big world out there Liz. What a lonesome place loving can be. It's touched me often but never quite allowed me to reach my destination, and you know me Liz, I always reach my destination."

Time was not on Cody's side. He did find a burning deep love that filled him with happiness and joy. He lived long enough

56

through his battle with leukemia to experience exactly what he was looking for – Me!

The day he passed away, he motioned me into his inner world for the last time. It was our third Christmas eve. With tears channeling down my face, I languished in front of a crackling fire, day dreaming of our days of love, and passion cut oh so short.

The view from our apartment overlooking Central Park was breathtaking. The falling snow glistened in the moonlight as it blanketed the Park in a frosted maze. "What a view," I thought. "How many times Cody and I walked hand-in-hand chilled to the bone, but our happy souls always smiled in our winter wonderland.

432 Park Avenue seemed like the closest thing to heaven."

For the first time I dreaded the opening of the bedroom door. The doctor came out with compassion in his eyes, touched my shoulder and told me Cory had little time left. My heart was throbbing so hard I could hardly breathe. "Please God just a few more minutes." I rushed to his bedside. Once again, he held my hand... and as usual I sat down and listened.

"Lizzie... I'm happier than I have ever been, I'm not empty anymore... I do love you girl, I always have. Marrying you was my best merger." He tried to squeeze my hand. A strained half-smile appeared; his eyes seemed to search for something above I could not see. I felt the warmth of his hand cool, and with a single sigh, the look of peace reached out for him. I knew in spirit we would always be together. We had to be.

57

For me, Cody was someone I could count on. A business friendship that in a short time turned into an inner fulfilled love. For a time we were lost in the vast sea of life. We were like two ships that pass in the night Longfellow refers too, with no lasting significance other than stolen precious moments of time in an office. Then, we willing unpacked each other's baggage and sorted it all out.

Our emotional and spiritual safe place, our do-over, turned into fleeting moments of time we had no control over. And now they can never be shared again.

Cupid's golden arrow hit its mark, and it was up to us both to make it work. And we did... Oh boy, did we make it work!

Roadmap – Lines of Change

by Jolee L. Price

The band was playing Happy Birthday as I blew out the last candle of the number one hundred perched on top of the cake. A round of applause from the guests in the banquet room ensued, mingled with shouts of "Yea," "All right" and "You go, Nana."

"Nana, it only took you three breaths," said my eight-year-old great-grandson, Nate.

I smiled but thought it would have only taken one breath if the genius who put the candles on the cake did not space eight to ten inches between each number.

As if reading my thoughts, Nate said, "Momma wanted me to put the numbers together Nana. She said it would be easier for you to blow out the candles, but I told her that you could do it." He pointed at the cake and continued, "I knew you could because you're a centurion."

My puzzled look caused Nate's immediate frown; poor Nate. He wanted so much to please me. Understanding fell into place. I took his hands in mine. "Oh Natey, you mean a centenarian. It's what they call a person who is one hundred years old or older."

Young defiance arose. "That's not what Mikey told me. He said that you were a centurion like the Roman centurions from the Bible."

Muffled snickers from the guests erupted into full-blown laughter. I snickered myself even though I relished in Nate's innocence.

Nate's twin brother, Mikey, ran toward the door. Nate, hot on his brother's heels, shouted, "You're in big trouble now!"

The party progressed. Cake was eaten. Gifts were opened. The band was playing.

I looked at my gifts. All were appreciated. However, carefully clipped to an easel was the epitome of a true centenarian's gift. It was a collage of pictures from my life reproduced on a royal blue afghan throw.

I traced the pictures with my fingers. Flickers of light from the banquet room's chandelier reflected on the mirrored wall beside me. My gaze followed the glistening lights and settled on my reflection. I peered closer. My lined face looked back. Those lines were showing my life's true pictorial roadmap, a foundation built on flesh with tears, defeat, and victory.

"Lines of change," I whispered.

If age worked in reverse, my face as a child would have been outlined with joy and laughter while being filled with lines of love. My parents taught my brother, sister and me by love and example. Rules were set down and kept without screaming or brutality. We were happy. I wanted that happiness to carry over into a family of my own.

I looked at the depth of my frown lines; the first one appeared in 1944. I married Jonathan, my high school sweetheart, in 1943, one month after graduation. He was ruggedly handsome in a Paul Bunyan kind of way. He had sandy-blond hair and brown eyes. Two months later, Jonathan enlisted in the army. He was killed in 1944. His death deepened the frown lines already etched from worry; stress-induced lines in the crooks of my eyes mingled with lines of joy from our brief time together.

I continued to work at Macy's in Cosmetics for the next few years. I was behind the cosmetic counter when I met my second future husband, Stefen, who eventually bought a bottle of cologne. His looks fit his profession; he was a successful plastic surgeon. He was movie-star handsome – tall with broad shoulders. His hair was midnight black, and he had eyes bluer than Paul Newman's. He was deceptively charming.

We soon married. I didn't know it at the time, but frown lines number two and three would make their appearance. His tyranny was subtle at first. He chose everything from where we lived to what we would buy and own. Even our social life was mapped out to his preference. He always said he wanted the best for us. Over the next five years, he turned his attention toward me personally, and I unintentionally became his client. His choices became more biased, molding and creating me into the image of what he wanted. I was becoming a by-product of my very own in-house Dr. Frankenstein. I was losing my identity physically and emotionally. I let the lure of money, and Stefen's false charms poach my ethics and self-esteem. My face reflected this in frown lines two and three.

Five years later, lines of frustration deepened across my forehead along with creases of stress around my eyes. His desire to change me, inwardly and outwardly, became constant. I refused to continue with his obsessive demands; I finally had enough. The day before I was going to meet an attorney, I was served with divorce papers. I thought Stefen had found out my plans. It was just the opposite. He was leaving me for a younger woman whose age would nearly constitute statutory rape. I was thirty-eight when we divorced.

Two years later, I met my best friend Frieda for dinner to celebrate my fortieth birthday. While Frieda went to the ladies' room, a young man approached me and said, "I had to come over and wish you a Happy Birthday."

After having been widowed and divorced, I wanted nothing more to do with love. Instead of thanking him, I blurted out, "I'm forty. I'm too old for you. Go away."

Without missing a beat, he replied, "I'm thirty. I teach math; therefore, I fear no decimals."

A demur cough elicited behind him. It was Frieda, who upon seeing Nathanial, could not wait to leave. She winked at me and left. Nathanial immediately asked to join me for coffee. I accepted. We talked for hours. Indeed, he was a math professor. I detected no arrogance from this humorous man. He had a yuppie look with his round wire-rimmed glasses and short brown tousled hair. Nothing nerdy about him at all; I thought he looked sexy.

I was forty-one when we married. I had our first child, Nathanial, Jr. when I was forty-two. Everyone we knew thought that I would have a difficult pregnancy because of my age. They were wrong.

I was forty-four when our twin daughters, Natalie and Sophia were born. Since everything went well with our son, everyone thought this pregnancy would be a repeat. We were all wrong. I was nauseated my entire pregnancy. I developed creases along the sides of mouth from frequent vomiting. I couldn't seem to gain weight. Saltines became a staple. Worry lines surfaced across my forehead.

A few months later when the twins started kicking, I wanted to kick back. I didn't realize I would be giving birth to two future high school soccer players. Through it all, Nathanial was my rock. He ultimately concocted a protein shake that wouldn't bow to morning sickness. It was a long nine months, but we made it.

I finally had my happy family. We lived life; oh, how we lived! We were married twenty-five years when Nathanial died in a car accident. He was only fifty-six. A drunk driver ran a stop sign.

The true love of my life was gone. Lines of grief and anger were joined by dark circles with matching bags under my eyes. Valium was my companion. My children, aged twenty-four and twenty-two, soon took over parenting me. Exercising tough love, they threw out my valium. When the numbness of the drug wore off, I realized the self-centeredness of my own grief. I lost my husband, but I had three children who had lost their father. They did not want to lose their mother.

It was difficult, sometimes seemingly impossible, but through love and example, we moved forward.

I looked at my seasoned face in the mirror and whispered, "And here we are."

"What are you looking at Nana?" asked Nate.

Hugging Nate, I answered, "Just an old roadmap Natey; just an old roadmap."

Ring Around

by Shannon Carroll

Her favorite part about visiting her grandma was getting to explore the forest behind her house. Sophia was allowed to walk through the forest, so long as she didn't wander too far and lose sight of her grandma's yellow cottage.

She was so glad to be back here. Years had passed since the last time she was allowed to visit her grandmother. A girl in town had died in an animal attack. Sophia's parents didn't think it was safe for her to visit anymore. The only reason she got to stay with her grandma now was because her dad had lost his job. Her parents didn't have the money to take care of her anymore. Mom said they were choosing "the lesser of two evils." She didn't like the idea of Sophia staying with her grandma, but she said they didn't have any better options.

Sophia didn't really understand what her mom meant. She didn't understand why she couldn't stay at home. Her parents were sending her away… because they loved her?

She didn't mind, though. Since her dad had lost his job, seeing her grandma again was one of the best things to happen to Sophia. Her parents were so strict and overprotective. The farthest they ever let Sophia go on her own was from one end of their block to the other.

Her grandma was the only adult who ever let her go off on

her own, and Sophia was grateful. She sometimes felt trapped at home. Her entire world was one block. When she was little, her family used to have a pet cat. She was just a kitten when they got her. She was always sitting in front of the glass door that led to their backyard, and anytime someone moved to go outside, she would follow right behind them. Yet every time, they'd shut the door with her still inside the house. They didn't want her to be an outdoor cat. Her parents said letting her outside would be too dangerous.

Years passed, and she became a fat old housecat. She still sat by the door sometimes, but she never tried to go out, not even when Sophia left the door wide open for her for a whole minute. Sophia realized that the feline had lost her taste for the world, and something seized painfully in her chest. She felt like the little kitten they'd adopted all those years ago was dead, and she hadn't even noticed until that moment. Ever since then, Sophia had a horrible, irrational fear that one day, she would become an indoor cat, too.

That morning, she pulled on an old pair of jeans and her favorite sweater, the one with the fuzzy cat on the front. She had to dress warm if she didn't want to catch a cold, or get scratched up by poison ivy. She hugged her grandma goodbye and went out to explore the forest. Humming contentedly, she skipped around the trees, looking for flowers to pick or stray animals to play with.

She stopped when she came to a ring of mushrooms. They formed a near-perfect circle on the ground. Amidst the gnarled

65

trees and the tangled bramble bushes, the mushroom ring appeared so… elegant. Sophia never thought she'd see something so exquisite in her wild forest. In the middle of the ring, there was a clean patch of grass. Perfect for planting something, like flowers for her grandma.

"You shouldn't be here by yourself." A sharp voice cut through her reverie. She looked up to see a girl not much older than her. She had on a red hood that stood out starkly against her pallid skin. "The forest is a dangerous place."

Sophia frowned at her. "It doesn't look very dangerous. Besides, my grandma's house is just a little ways down." She pointed to where her grandma's cottage stood just at the edge of the forest. "I'm perfectly safe here."

The girl looked put out. "That's what I said," she muttered, but Sophia was no longer listening to her. She was stepping closer to the mushroom circle, looking to see how much space she had to work with.

"Don't get too close! That's a faerie ring."

"A what?" Sophia looked up at her with an annoyed glare.

"A faerie ring." The girl looked down at her, equally annoyed. "It's a trap that faeries leave for humans. If you step into it, they'll force you to dance with them until you die."

Sophia made a big show of rolling her eyes. She was smart enough not to believe every story she heard. "I don't believe in faeries. I don't believe in Santa Claus, either, by the way." She

66

stepped past the girl and made her way to the circle.

"Stop!" The girl jumped in front of Sophia, blocking her path. Undeterred, Sophia kept going. She'd spent enough time getting told what to do by her parents; she wasn't about to get told what to do by this random person. She was prepared to barrel right through the bossy girl, if she had to.

She didn't. Not quite, anyway; she didn't barrel through the girl so much as walk through her, as easy as a knife sliding through hot butter. As easy as if the girl weren't a girl at all, but a fog; a mist; a ghost. Sophia gasped. She windmilled her arms about, trying to turn herself around. But she had been going too fast as she tried to make her way past the other girl. Even with her arms swinging about, she couldn't stop herself from stumbling backwards into the faerie ring.

The strange ghost-girl quickly disappeared from her mind. As soon as she entered the ring, she felt hands wrap around her, solid and insistent. They pulled her in further until she was surrounded by men – men with wings on their backs and leers on their faces. They swung her around until she was dizzy; so dizzy, she felt like she'd collapse without them holding her up. Were these men faeries? She didn't understand what was happening. The men were laughing and jeering so loud, she couldn't think. She couldn't see her grandma's cottage anymore.

She could see the sky above her and the trees that made up the forest, but only barely; like she was peering through a telescope or a long tunnel or a distant window on a foggy day. She was

67

floating, disconnected from the world but still close enough to watch it go on without her. She could have sworn only a moment passed; yet, she knew herself to be wrong. Above her, the sky changed colors and the trees lost their leaves. With each passing second, the seasons flickered by. She blinked; it was winter. The ground was encased in a fine sheet of snow.

These demons were going to dance with her until she died. And it wouldn't take very long.

Her heart seized in her chest. Her poor grandmother. How long would she wait for Sophia to come back? How long would she grieve for her? How deeply would her heart break, when she realized that her granddaughter was dead and she hadn't even noticed? But then, Sophia realized, the police would never find her body. Maybe her grandma would convince herself that Sophia had run away. Her parents would no doubt assume she'd gotten eaten by a wolf, but maybe her grandma would believe she was out there somewhere, alive and well.

The sky turned purple, like a dark, violent bruise. Snow melted into rain. It fell from the clouds and splattered onto her upturned face. A puddle quickly gathered at the center of the circle, where the ground dipped. The faeries stomped and thrashed about in it; sprays of water flew out every which way.

Some of it soaked her pants. Some of it landed just outside the ring. Sophia gasped, an idea forming in her mind. The faerie ring wasn't impermeable from the inside. If the rain could find a way out, then so could she.

The next time one of the men spun her around, she took advantage of the momentum she was given. She ripped her hand out of his hold and leapt forward, hands reached out in a desperate bid for safety.

She landed in a heap along the ring's perimeter. She could feel a mushroom wedged under her elbow. A rough hand grabbed her ankle, threatening to drag her back in.

"No!" she screamed. She dug her nails into the ground, trying to claw herself out of the trap. "Help! Can anybody hear me? Help!"

The strange girl materialized in front of her. "Take my hand!"

Could she? The last time she'd gone to touch the girl, Sophia had passed right through her. She didn't know; but the other girl seemed so sure, so certain that she could help, if only Sophia reached out.

She offered a dirty hand to the girl. When their hands met, they passed right through each other; little fingers wrapped around nothing.

Sophia cried out.

"Try again." The girl wiggled her fingers at Sophia, encouraging her to grab on.

She did. This time, her hand didn't fall through. The strange girl felt as solid as any of the men pulling at her. She swung her legs about wildly, trying to break loose from their grip. One of them made a pained grunt; then she was out of the ring, half crawling and half being dragged by the other girl.

She landed in a tangle of limbs on the ground. The other girl fell beside her. "Believe me now?" There wasn't a bit of smugness in her voice.

As soon as Sophia got up, she looked down at herself, checking her body for injuries. Her clothes were ripped. At first, she thought the rips were because of the men pulling at her, but then she noticed something. Her shirt fell an inch above her belly button; her pants no longer reached her ankles.

She met the girl with a horrified gaze. "How long was I in there?"

There was a long pause before she answered. "A year. I thought you would be in there longer," she added, quickly, like a mother trying to soothe an injured child. "Most people never escape the faerie rings; or if they do, so much time has passed by then that they turn into a pile of ash the moment they escape."

"A year," Sophia repeated, in a hushed, horrified whisper.

"I tried to warn you," the girl said, in a soft voice. "I died in this forest. I was acting careless and foolish, like a child. Now I try to stop other people from repeating my mistakes." She scowled, like she was angry with herself for allowing herself to die.

"You are a child," Sophia said.

"Not anymore."

Sophia looked back at her ruined clothes. A part of her wanted to change right away, but another part wanted to cry at the thought of losing her favorite sweater. She felt like a new person. Someone strange and gawky that she didn't recognize. Someone she wasn't ready to become yet. She felt like she didn't fit into her own skin anymore. She had outgrown herself, and she wasn't ready. Her voice sounded scratchy when she spoke. "Me neither."

***

Years later, she came back to visit her grandma one more time.

Her grandma never understood why Sophia disappeared that day. Neither did her parents. She didn't know how to explain to them what had happened to her. Faeries; lost time; ghost girls. She couldn't wrap her head around it all. If she couldn't understand it all for herself, how could she ever begin to explain it to anyone else?

After that day, she never got to visit her grandma again. Her parents signed her up for counselling. They never knew exactly what had happened to their daughter, but they knew it was something bad. Sophia was different when she came back. More than just her body had changed. For months, she wouldn't leave the house at all. She would get as close as the front door, and then, with one foot raised over the threshold, she'd start sobbing uncontrollably.

She had to grow up all over again. Baby steps: one day, she made it past the front door. Weeks passed before she found the nerve to do it again. Yet more weeks before she made it to the end of the driveway. The day she was able to walk around her block by herself, she knew she was going to be okay.

It helped that she had a secret weapon. Her father had given it to her a month or two after she came back. At the time, Sophia still couldn't make it out the front door. Her parents were getting desperate. One day, her dad sat with her and asked her what she needed from him. He phrased it exactly that way: 'What do you need from me?' Sophia's dad was never much of a talker. He didn't go out of his way to meet people. He barely made small talk with their neighbors; when Sophia came back, she was a more of a stranger to him than they were.

He didn't know how to talk to her anymore. But since he'd gotten a new job, he could certainly buy things for her; if nothing else than to make up for the time he couldn't.

'What do you need from me?'

She told him. It wasn't much. Just one thing: it was as small as a stone, and it fit inside her pocket. She carried it everywhere with her. It was her lucky charm; her security blanket. Her father had given her a strange look when she asked for it, but he didn't ask questions.

To this day, she never left the house without it. Going back to school had been so strange. She felt somehow younger and older than all of her classmates. She was behind on the curriculum; she

72

still wore sweaters with fuzzy animals on them, while the rest of her class had moved onto boring sweatshirts and yoga pants; some of the people in her grade even had learner's permits, while Sophia got dropped off by her parents every day because she couldn't stomach the idea of being trapped in the crowded bus. Everyone else was ahead of her in life. She didn't know how to make friends anymore: she didn't understand the jokes people made or the lingo they used with their friends. Like, sometimes in the hallway, a person would see their friend at their locker and hide behind the locker door to scare them. As soon as the person closed their locker, the other person jumped out and screamed hello at them. It was a game people played, to see how much they could scare their friends. That was one of the times she felt older than everyone else at her school. All of her classmates acted so reckless and carefree and immature. Sophia didn't want a friend that would sneak up on her and make her scream bloody murder.

There were times when she wondered if she would ever fit in with other people again. There were times when she wondered if she even wanted to. Mostly, there were times when she wanted to give up and stay at home forever. During those times, she would reach into her pocket and clutch her lucky charm; she would remind herself she'd been through much worse things than high school.

She squeezed it now, as she walked toward that old yellow cottage by herself. Her parents had refused to come with her. She reminded herself she'd been through worse than even this.

She could do this. She was an adult now. She lived on her

own. She had a degree in Mythology and Folklore. Soon she would go to graduate school and get her Master's, and then she would move onto teaching. She was excited to be teaching, not because she got to regale students with intriguing fairytales, but because she got to warn them about the world's very real hidden dangers.

Grandma had died in an animal attack. Wolves. Sophia brought flowers, clutched in the hand that wasn't fisted in her pocket.

Not many other people came to the wake. Her grandma lived in a small town. Sophia guessed most people were laying low after the animal attack.

She had hoped the ghost girl might show up. But she never did. At the end of the ceremony, Sophia went back out to the forest behind her grandma's house. Her grandmother had requested that her ashes be spread there.

Just the same as all those years ago, she felt herself being drawn to the faerie ring. It was just as she remembered, though she didn't remember it well. Her time in the faerie ring was a blur to her. But she remembered the strange perfectness of the circle. She remembered the bed of grass she'd considered planting flowers in.

She wasn't as afraid of it as she thought she might be. Though, that was the trick with enchanted things. They had a certain charm about them; a certain intrigue. She had learned to understand beauty as a warning sign. Any good trap came with a good lure.

"You shouldn't be here by yourself." Sophia tried not to jump. She was jumpy at the best of times, and ghosts had an unfair advantage when it came to catching people off guard.

She was exactly the same as Sophia remembered. Sophia looked older than her now.

"I know," she said. She was wise enough to be aware of all the dangers she couldn't see. The world was fraught with unseen peril and tragedy. She had no guarantee of safety. "My grandma died."

"I know. I'm sorry."

"Did you–?"

"I saw her. I'm sorry," she repeated. "I tried to help her."

"I know you did. Just like you helped me." Sophia had never gotten the chance to thank her for saving her. But she'd thought about her a lot in the years since. This strange ghost girl was the only person in the world who understood what she'd been through. "You never told me your name."

"Rory." She didn't offer Sophia a handshake. She didn't smile as she introduced herself. They weren't exchanging pleasantries; Sophia wasn't asking her name to be polite. This was something much bigger than small talk; this was conversation. She wanted to know who this girl was that saved her all those years ago. Rory knew this. She took a deep breath, as if steadying her nerves. "A long time ago, I was killed by a wolf. It was from the same pack as the one that took your grandmother. I wanted more than anything to be able to save her from my fate. But I failed her, and now I'm afraid I'll never know peace."

Sophia realized with a start that this girl was the closest thing she had to a friend. They understood each other in a way no one else did. She opened her mouth to say something; but before she could, she saw something move out of the corner of her eye.

A wolf. He stared back at her with big eyes. Slowly, he stalked forward, towards the two of them. He wasn't close to them yet, but she could already hear the growl in his throat. Low and predatory.

Rory stepped in front of her. Her voice was sharpened steel. "Walk away slowly. Don't do anything to draw his attention."

Slowly, Sophia took a few steps towards her grandma's old cottage.

The wolf snarled and snapped his jaws at her. She froze.

"I'm going to try and distract him," Rory said. She hurried towards where the wolf was standing. A few paces behind him, she snapped a stick, trying to catch his attention.

His eyes never strayed from Sophia. He appeared to have picked his target, and he wasn't changing his focus anytime soon. He stepped closer; those big eyes threatened to swallow her whole.

Sophia took a step back.

"Stop!"

Her breath caught in her throat. Looking behind her, she

saw that she was mere inches away from the faerie ring.

The wolf stalked closer.

"What should I do?" she cried.

Rory seemed to be at a loss. "You could try running to your grandma's cottage. I'll do what I can to hold him back." She sounded suddenly scared and uncertain, so unlike the headstrong girl Sophia knew.

Headstrong people only ever sounded uncertain when they were completely out of options. It was the same way her mother had sounded when she told a young Sophia she was going to live with her grandmother.

Cautiously, Sophia raised one foot over the edge of the faerie ring. Tears were pouring down her face; she ignored them.

"What are you doing?" Rory cried.

She would never get to her grandma's cottage in time. The wolf was bigger and faster and stronger than her. The world was fraught with unseen dangers. She had no guarantee of safety. Sometimes, you were left with no solid footing. No safe harbor. And in those times, you needed to choose a tragedy you could live with; a storm you could weather.

So; the vicious beast, or the possessive faeries? The one who hurt her grandmother, or the ones who kept Sophia as their prized captive? The one who would eat her whole, or the ones who made her feel like she was nothing, nothing but a toy to be played with

77

till it broke?

Gone was that idealistic girl she'd been so many years ago. Faeries were real. Grandmothers could be wrong. Her parents had always done the best they could to love her. Sophia understood now. "I'm choosing the lesser of two evils," she said.

With a snap of his teeth, the wolf lunged for her.

She let herself fall back into the faerie ring.

A hand grabbed her arm. She ripped away from the grip, pulling something out of her pocket. She squeezed it. She would be okay. She had been through worse than even this.

She didn't look up to watch the seasons change. She didn't mourn the loss of time. When she next stepped out of the ring, maybe things would be better. Maybe the world would look a little brighter. Maybe wolves would stop eating girls. Maybe faeries would stop playing cruel tricks. Maybe Rory would finally know peace. Maybe girls would be girls, and not ghosts; maybe men would be men, and not beasts.

She showed them what she had pulled from her pocket. Her secret weapon. It was a piece of iron. She never left the house without it.

The faeries flinched away from it. Gone was the mischievous twinkle from their eyes. Gone was the mirth, gone was the charm; gone was the lure they used to hide their trap. Their faces contorted with anger. They turned away and screamed at her.

She stepped out of the faerie ring, just as quickly as she'd stepped in. The screaming cut off all at once. It gave way to heavy silence.

The wolf had left. She was safe. The sun was rising. She could smell the scent of flowers in the air. It smelled like spring.

Rory was waiting for her.

"How much time have I lost?" Sophia asked her.

"Just a few months." Rory offered her a smile, though it looked pained. Just a few months. She wondered what she was going to tell her parents.

It took her a moment to summon the right words. Words that would make this better. In the end, she couldn't find them. She settled for words that wouldn't make it any worse. "Better than my life, I suppose."

She clutched the iron in her fist.

"Better than your life," Rory agreed.

Stardust

by Carolyn Hill

"Babies are bits of stardust blown from the hand of God," according to playwright Larry Barretto. You and I are two of them. Our lives are patterned like the seasons. We learn and grow, plant our seeds of hope and ultimately reap what we sow. Supposedly, 10% of life's changes are what happens to us and 90% is how we react.

Do you realize your first cry in the delivery room was the beginning "season" in the revolving cycle of your life? Think of it as a springtime moment where you, like the dormant season of winter, emerge into existence out of a sleepy darkness in an amazing escape from Nature's womb. With a gasp for fresh air you catapult as the early morning Crocus, to announce a precious child of God with a little bald head has arrived to tackle the symphony of life.

Amazing how everything moves in perfect harmony with everything else by Divine design. Babies will cry within seconds if they are not immediately reunited with their mother. They are the only ones who intimately know Mom by the beat of her heart.

Each new cooing star becomes part of an over-lapping story of many stories; mysteries yet to be unraveled. Where will that first dominant cry lead baby in a world of starts and ends? Here, in my arms, to simply take my breath away.

An anonymous soul once penned: "A baby fills a place in your heart you never knew was empty." Pop rock star Jordan Taylor Hanson was quoted in *Cosmopolitan*, "It gives you a whole other perspective on why you get up every day."

Can you see it... the immense cuteness and innocence of a baby's glowing gift of love? It's sent from heaven you know. There's an unquestioning smile resting amid chubby little cheeks and shiny pink flesh, and you melt. Love fills your heart and the world is good.

One thing for sure, a baby will always be a contradiction of life even before the mind is lit by the fire of knowledge. There is a truism, "A baby makes love stronger, the days shorter, the nights longer, savings smaller, and a home happier." This bundle of minority rule can turn its occupants' lives upside-down, then do something to tickle the heart and ignite the embers of love.

Suddenly you are shaking your head in amazement. For before you is a piece of your flesh and spirit. A little slugger who always has a pocket full of mischief to share, or sweetness in pink filled with smiles, and giggles, and pure delight, like rainbow bubbles floating on air.

Ecclesiastes 3:1-2 reminds us, "For everything there is an appointed time, even a time for every affair under the heavens: a time for birth and a time to die; a time to plant and a time to uproot what was planted."

Like all of us, step by step, baby will learn and test the seasons of the never-ending circle from childhood to the childhood of old age and expiring time.

The Hunt Starts at Sunrise

by James Pressler

Steve clenched his rifle tight against his chest, shielding it from the tree branches swiping at him from the pre-dawn shadows. This was his favorite rifle, Bolt. He named it because it wasn't just some hardware to hang by a strap on his shoulder. He protected it like a cherished friend while guiding the hunting party through the woods.

"Dammit, Steve," Ted shouted from behind him. "Warn me about those branches flying at me. I can barely see as is, and one of those things is gonna cost me an eye!"

"Maybe stop walking on my heels. If you was up any closer, you'd be in my damn backpack!"

"Shhh!" Zeke scolded from the back of the group.

"Don't go shhhing me," Ted snapped back in a much softer tone. "Just trying to let this guy know there's someone behi—"

A branch swept off Steve's torso and slapped Ted across the mouth.

"Branch," Steve warned sarcastically.

"Keep it down," Zeke scolded in a loud whisper.

Ted rubbed his face. "Dammit, do you even know where you're going, Steve? I swear, if you get us all lost on the first day of hunting season, you'll be the one we're shooting at."

"I know where I'm going." Steve pushed aside some undergrowth, wading through thorny vines grabbing at his canvas pants. "I scouted out this place days ago. It's just a little harder to find at night."

"Harder to find? You got us lost, didn't you?"

"I'm the outdoorsman," Steve fired back. "Me and Bolt've been doing this all my life without nobody's help, so don't go snapping at me because you decided you'd join us this year but didn't expect it to be tough. Should I've warned you you'd get mud on your boots on your first hunt?"

"I've hunted before," Ted declared. "Not like this one, but birds and such."

"Sure." Steve stopped to face Ted, who was little more than an undersized shadow in the woods. "That's no bird-shooting rifle you got. Who brings an automatic rifle on a hunting trip? You looking to bag everything before anyone else gets a shot off?"

Ted held his rifle out. "Quick bursts guarantee a kill."

Steve shook his head and held out Bolt, emphasizing its long, pronounced barrel. "On this hunt, it's all about one shot, one kill. Old Bolt here is a long-bore, bolt-action..."

Zeke stepped between them. "Boys, put 'em back in your pants and save the bragging for once the sun rises. Steve, you said we'd meet Dave and Preacher at this spot of yours, right?"

Steve nodded.

"Good. Let's go. I want to settle in before sun-up." Zeke gestured forward and Steve again took the lead, fighting through the brush.

"I've got more muzzle velocity," Ted said defiantly.

"Shhh!" Zeke hissed.

A cell phone chimed through the pre-dawn mist.

"Oops," Zeke said. "My bad. One sec."

Zeke took the call and spent the next few minutes only saying, "Yes, dear," and, "I'm already at the hunting site, dear," repeatedly. The call ended with a fatigued, "I'm turning off the phone, dear," as he disconnected, shaking his head.

"The little woman again?" Steve asked.

"Yeah-huh." Zeke turned off his phone and tucked it deep in his pack. "She wanted to get in one last round of all the 'so cruel' and 'they're all God's creatures' noise. Let's just go."

Steve pushed forward. "Did you ever explain to her about population control? Thinning the herd? Keeping the numbers down for the good of the others"

"Did you ever tell her to shut her yapper?" Ted added.

"She ain't never gone hunting, she's never going hunting, and that's that with that. It ain't gonna change."

"You tried," Steve said. "Branch..."

"What?" A branch smacked Ted in the face.

84

The night sky was in full retreat as Steve, Ted, and Zeke approached their destination. They had all smelled coffee five minutes earlier, and it guided them the rest of the way. They emerged from the heavy undergrowth to find Dave and Preacher leaning against a felled tree, sharing a Thermos of coffee.

"Sorry we're late," Steve said. "A little tricky in the dark, and with Zeke's wife calling and all…"

Preacher raised his cup to them. "No matter. Glad you made it. Nice spot, by the way. Maybe this came down during that storm last spring."

The downed tree trunk was three feet wide and came down right by the tree line. If it had fallen any other direction it would've been useless as a hunting blind, but this position was perfect, providing ideal space to hide and a line of sight across the clearing.

Steve and Zeke set down their gear and chose positions. Ted was still looking around when Dave spoke up.

"Kinda red in the face, Ted. Them guys rough you up on the way here?"

"Nothing. Night hiking. Dumb-ass tree branches."

"Yep," Dave said. "First time I came out here, those thorn bushes tore my legs raw. It's always something."

Ted put his gear by Dave. "Really? How many years have you done this hunt?"

"This'd be six for me."

"Baker's dozen here," Preacher added.

"And we've done ten each," Steve said, gesturing at Zeke as well.

"And... well, do you have any... many kills?"

"Seventeen clean ones for me," Preacher said, "and six where I got a hit but I didn't bag it because it wasn't the kill shot."

"Thirteen, all clean," Dave answered.

"Twenty-one," Zeke said without any emphasis.

"Twelve," Steve said, tapping his rifle. "All with good old Bolt here."

Ted sat down, accepting a cup of Thermos coffee from Preacher. "Okay then, I've only hunted birds and stuff. What's this like? What's that first real kill like?"

Dave sat up. "Not much, really. Like the first time I bagged an elk. I pulled the trigger and it went down. It was alive, then it wasn't. Nothing different here. It's pretty simple."

Preacher nodded. "If you're uncomfortable with it, think of it as a merciful act. These animals don't control their environment, they overrun it. They burden it at the expense of everything else. In the larger picture, it's for their own good."

"Don't worry," Zeke added. "On your first hunt, you'll be lucky to even get one."

"Hey, I'm a good shot!" Ted protested, holding up his rifle.

Steve smirked. "Yeah, assuming that automatic doesn't spray your lead all over the field. You'll have a dry clip before you can take aim."

"I'm telling you…"

"Never you two mind," Zeke interrupted. "Ted, look along our tree line. You can't see them, but there's plenty of people in those shadows, ready to do exactly what you're aiming to do. Nice weather means maybe a hundred hunters waiting for the crack of dawn, begging to bag the first one of the season. A hundred hunters might be on the light side, actually. Even with bad weather, the guns outnumber those animals. Just have patience, let them come, pick one you want to bag, and let it happen. You'll have bragging rights soon enough." Zeke pointed at him. "And don't shoot the first one out of the grass. Every young, loose-triggered newbie goes for that one. Let them train on that. Just wait and it'll happen."

"Thanks." Ted nestled against the fallen tree, resting his arm against a broken branch for support and bringing around the rifle. Everyone took their spots, eyes focused on the high grasses at the far end of the clearing.

The eastern clouds glowed red with the morning sun approaching. Soon they would hear the whistle blow, declaring the opening of hunting season.

***

Inside the walls of Wakefield Prison, sixty men in orange jumpsuits stood by the closed steel gates, some nervously fidgeting in place, others trying to peek through the gate and beyond the security perimeter. When the loudspeaker came to life, they all fell silent.

This is the Warden. For the first time in your worthless lives, I applaud the choice you all have made that brings you to this courtyard. As prisoners condemned to life sentences, you could have spent the rest of your time feeding off a state that considers you unworthy of freedom. However, you have made a noble decision, choosing to take control of your lives and relieve the state of the burden that is you.

When the gates open, you must leave the prison's property at once. You become men without a state, without rights or freedoms, and without refuge. If you reach the river and cross the border, this country is no longer concerned about your existence and you may seek asylum as you see fit. However, between the time you leave here and the time you find some other place to call home, you are without legal protection. You are not citizens. You are not people. You are nothing more than animals in the eyes of the state, and will be treated accordingly. Seek freedom, and may God have mercy on your souls.

With a wrenching groan, the steel gates cracked open. The prisoners shielded their eyes from the brilliance of the just-rising sun, then ran out of the prison, down the road, and toward the clearing outside the prison's property.

As they came over the first hill, the hunters opened fire.

The Fifth Dimension

by Carolyn Hill

Mankind finds himself captivated by life, like the enchanting optical illusion of the autumn harvest moon, which isn't orange at all. The world is his oyster, but not always for the taking. As the earth keeps spinning, the day comes and goes. Suddenly his world crashes to a stop. In helplessness he begins to wonder, "Lord, where are you?"

Man's personal growth is like the whims of Mother Nature. They both bloom in the days of warmth and the calmness of life. They struggle through the difficult times, but it is man alone, who can be blinded when doing what so many do... resort to human reasoning. Ecclesiastes 3:1 is a reminder: "...to everything there is a season, and a time for every purpose under the heavens."

Man is no exception. What a magnificent creature. His spirit is eager, yet the will is weak. Life becomes a personal journey of endurance against the endless storms that come, with no letup from birth until the last fainting breath. His accomplishments capture our attention with the material and the extraordinary; yet he has proven an inability to rule himself since the beginning of time.

It has been millenniums since Adam and Eve succumbed to the evil that now runs rampant throughout the earth. Man seems to be in perpetual osmosis like the nature of springtime, fickle and unstable.

89

Distracted by trivial pursuits and discouraged by hardships and self-inflicted pain, this magnificent creation called man, struggles to balance his life, but peace and contentment never comes. At some point, he seeks something greater than himself. ... He yearns in confusion and dreams in hope of something more wonderful than what he has. As he searches his inner being his heart cries out - his mind questions: "Lord, are you real?"

Perhaps that hope of perfection and a higher power does exist. Look upward... In suspension the stars twinkle like diamonds. They flutter with red, heated by the mysterious cosmic gases. In their coolness others sparkle with the vibrant color of the ocean's blue depth. In harmony, they orchestrate their own symphony of pulsating beauty that dots the darkened heavens for the world to see.

This ethereal part of the Milky Way didn't just happen. Its breathtaking mastery seems to awaken the emotions of the heart. Yet, throughout man's search he repeats the same mind-boggling question, "Lord, what is the purpose of my existence?"

Some people believe in a higher power, but not the God of the Bible. It seems there would be no greater treasure to be found than the answers to man's search of why he exists and what the future holds for the earth and all of mankind. Try as we may, none of us on our own can escape the ultimate physical enemy ... death! – 1 Corinthians 15:26

Have you ever asked God for rescue, even though you weren't sure he exists? Why? Can the Bible be trusted? If yes, it would be foolish…if not fatal…to ignore it during these "end times," of which it speaks. How can you decide? Perhaps test Him, and with an open mind like the Bereans'(Acts 17:11), search the written Word to find out if it is the inspired of God, and not simply the words of men.

Like any other proof, intriguing evidence exists about its historical accuracy as revealed millenniums before Science, Astronomy, Archeology, Geology, and Paleontology learned about them.

And so, the search for an answer comes full circle, from optimism to pessimism and back again. Is this life all there is? Is there another dimension to come after death? If there is, what will man do with what he learns while he searches for the truth of his existence.

The famous educator William Lyon Phelps was quoted in the *New Dictionary of Thought,* page 46, "I believe … knowledge of the Bible without a college course is more valuable than a college course without a Bible."

Is it just a hopeful dream to find all that is perfect? I too want to know there is more to life than humanity crashing headlong against each other. What is your Shangri-La, a state of mind, a paradise amidst the chaos of the world or the faith fulfillment of a biblical Garden of Eden. In that dimension, the Good Book tells of a place, "Where righteousness dwells and the turbulent 'sea' of wicked rebellious mankind will cease to exist" - 2:Peter 3:13

Imagine the kind of authority that could command the earth to burst forth with every imaginable beauty and needed provision of life. Where the dust of the desert is swept away and the heat-parched ground of the wilderness thrives as springs of water (Isaiah 35:1,6,7) Here, an ageless man will find peace, possessing the earth free from war, hunger, poverty, pain, sickness and the every flowing tears of heartbreak of this world. - Psalm 46:9; 37:28,29; Isaiah 33:24

Once again, science and philosophy interact with the idea that the "Earth and all beings living on the planet are shifting into a whole new level of reality called a 5th Dimension consciousness of love, joy, peace, freedom, compassion, and where spiritual wisdom prevails," according to sciencing.com.

And yet, though man seems to hunger for the way of knowledge and truth, he seems sidetracked by the genius of science, not paying attention that such spiritual knowledge already exists within the 66 books of the Bible.

It's all about choice. Opening the heart is the key to understanding what or who guides us in regards to our existence and unseen realities. The curves of learning not only answer man's questions, but teaches us how to "make sure of all things; hold fast to what is fine," according to 1 Thessalonians 5:21.

Consider, the written Word like a massive puzzle of great intrigue. God hides a little piece of the story here and a little there. His puzzle once put together allows us to understand the how and why, any of us may be seduced by the doctrines of men.

Springing Into A New Career

by Colin Kirchner

Who knew that going back to college at the age of forty would be such a long, drawn-out undertaking? I had an epiphany that I wanted to do something different. Emptiness and uncertainty permeated my world. My marriage of fifteen years was on the rocks, my computer programming job at a marketing research company left my soul empty, and I wanted to work with people, not computers.

My epiphany made me feel like a teenager again once I figured out what I wanted to do for the rest of my life. Initially, I wanted to become a Unitarian Universalist minister. I had recently started going back to church and cherished the support and spiritual guidance of our minister. Delivering my first lay sermon at the church was both exciting and daunting, and yet I wanted to go back and do it again.

With my newfound enthusiasm, I visited Meadville-Lombard Seminary in Chicago and really liked it there. I wanted to take a class and find out more about becoming a minister. A year later, I attended a course in religious humanism. The subject matter fascinated me, and I enjoyed getting to know the seminary students. I finished the class and considered my next move. While I liked the idea of leading a church and encouraging spiritual growth, my faith dwindled once my divorce became finalized. I felt despair due to the death of my marriage and knowing I would not

93

be involved with my children every day.

My dream of being a minister faded as emptiness filled my soul. Even so, I craved change and wanted to pursue a different career working with people instead of computers. After talking with a psychologist friend from church and reflecting on how therapy had helped me through rough patches in my life, I decided to explore a career in counseling.

Feeling nervous yet determined about starting a new journey, I visited the admissions counselor at Governors State University. Before I could be admitted to the master's level counseling program, I had to take an abnormal psychology class at the local community college. That fall, I enrolled in that class and learned about mental disorders such as depression, schizophrenia, and bipolar disorder. Our professor discussed her experiences working in a mental health clinic and treating patients. I really enjoyed writing papers, conducting research, and learning the class material. My love for psychology and helping others seemed like a perfect match for counseling.

After completing the abnormal psychology class, I enrolled in a Master of Counseling program. The university offered three courses of study: school counseling, marriage and family counseling, and clinical mental health. Initially, I wanted to pursue school counseling, but the requirements seemed unreasonable. I avoided the Marriage and Family Counseling track. After a nasty divorce, the last thing I wanted to do was work with couples in trouble. After some consideration, I chose to work with individuals and follow the clinical mental health path.

Attending graduate school was much more interesting than my undergraduate studies. I enjoyed reading the textbooks and participating in interactive classes. I liked learning about group counseling, career counseling, and famous psychologists. Sigmund Freud, Carl Jung, Virginia Satir, and William Glasser became my new mentors. I felt awkward being one of the oldest students in class, but I soon got over it and made friends. Going to class became the highlight of my week, outside of spending time with my kids. Learning a new trade gave me a new purpose and filled the void created by my divorce.

Each semester, I completed one or two classes while working at my computer job, and parenting my sons. In my last two years of school, my life took an upswing. I was close to graduating, travelled to California on vacation with my kids, started dating someone, and found a roommate. In addition, I loved a child and adolescent counseling class so much that I switched to the Marriage and Family Counseling track.

Sadly, my joy was short-lived. In the fall, I came down with pneumonia and took three months to recover. Writing my final paper focusing on emotionally-focused couples counseling was really difficult since it reminded me of my failed marriage. My relationship with my girlfriend ended, and I worried that I would miss my college friends once we graduated. Worst of all, I could no longer stand being around my roommate, who had lost his job and car and had no prospects of moving out. In addition, my boss told me that my computer job was going to be eliminated and, I had no idea how I was going to support myself while finishing school. My anxiety became so severe that I thought I was going insane.

I nearly lost faith that I could complete my internship and final year of school. My saving grace was befriending a coworker who cheered me on, reassuring me that I could handle the stress and succeed. Every morning, I worked at my job, not knowing when I would be fired. In the afternoons, I rode the train to my internship feeling exhausted and incredibly overwhelmed. I had a really hard time applying what I learned in class to my experience working with clients. Life at home was not much better.

My situation with my roommate continued to spiral down. I arrived home at night exhausted, wanting peace, only to be annoyed by the TV blaring and the smell of my roommate's cigarettes looming in the air. For a year, I repeatedly talked to my roommate about him finding a job and moving out. He offered one empty promise after another. My home became a place of torture rather than solace.

Through perseverance and determination, I completed my internship and celebrated by traveling to Scotland for a counseling convention. I loved getting away and felt overjoyed that I did not have to wear a kilt. Over the next few months, I continued working as counseling contractor while finishing the last two months of my computer job. My life seemed to be settling down, and yet my anxiety attacks continued. In order to graduate, I needed to finish my portfolio and pass an oral defense. I had an extremely difficult time assembling my portfolio, yet I completed it and successfully passed my defense. I felt ecstatic about graduating, but something was still not right.

My final hurdle was reclaiming my home. I gave my roommate an eviction notice, stating he had to leave before the new year. His empty promises of moving continued, so I took matters into my own hands. I talked with my friends and found someone who wanted a boarder. My roommate moved away, and I felt a huge sense of relief. Over the next few months, my panic attacks decreased as I settled in to my new counseling career.

After ten years of study, I earned my Master's degree in marriage and family counseling and accomplished my dream of becoming a therapist. My nightmares about getting divorced and feeling burnt out in my computer job faded. I felt renewed beginning my near career at age fifty, and like I was experiencing the second spring of my life.

Fishing Is My Favorite Hobby, Especially Ice Fishing!

by R. Patrick Brown

I have enjoyed fishing from the very first time that I went with my friend Ronnie, to the Sherman Park Lagoon in Chicago when I was eight years old. We only had three fishing hooks which we found on the edge of the water, after we finished flying kites in the park. We used some of our kite string and put hooks on two pieces of about seven feet of string and tied them to six-foot-long branches. Afterwards, we dug up some grass and found a few worms, which we put on the hooks as bait. Then we held the branches over the water and lowered the baited hooks into the water. After a short time, we each caught a very small fish. Ronnie caught the first and largest of the two. We both felt very excited about our successful pioneering experience. I guess you could say this was the beginning of my lifelong fishing hobby.

Since that day, I have fished on various rivers and lakes plus the Gulf of Mexico and even in the Atlantic Ocean. During leisure times in my life I have found these adventures to be very enjoyable and gratifying. The first time I ice fished was in December of 1967, I was with my friend Bill. We caught an assortment of 50 fish that day, which were mostly panfish, 8 to 10 inches or longer; plus two small Northern Pike. After that day, ice fishing became my preferred hobby and something I always looked forward to doing each winter. Another explanation of why ice fishing is my most loved hobby, is every time I have gone with others on frozen lakes in Illinois and Wisconsin I have caught five or more fish. Of course, there have been other jubilant ice fishing excursions that have kept me hooked on these fantastic experiences. One of them will be revealed instantly and different things will be disclosed later in this tale. On one such trip my wife Rita, and four of our children Kim, Sheri, Mike, Dawn and I along with friends, Bill and Teri, we caught a total of over 200 fish in less than 3 hours. What a fantastic day that was!

I believe, when there is a fresh layer of snow that it is a beautiful sight, because it covers most of the trash, debris and dormant plant life in fields, neighborhoods as well as countryside locations by farms, highway roads, parks and trees - making things picturesque. Another reason I love ice fishing is there are no mosquitoes, or other annoying insects...bothering me while I fish. Therefore, winter has become my most enjoyable season of the year. Other reasons that make winter the prize-winning season are: 1) fishing from a boat in turbulent water is likely to cause me to become dizzy and sick to my stomach. I have been told that these conditions are similar to motion/sea sickness; 2) not catching any fish on many trips while fishing during other seasons or the scorching heat of the summer sun and its reflection from the water that intensifies the burning of my fair skin; most people choose to start winter fishing when the lakes have been checked and declared safe for ice fishing season then go and find a place to set up the ice shanty or tent; to block the wind and other elements of winter weather. Then, we use a snow shovel and hand auger (hand auger is a tool used to cut a hole in the ice) to clear an area of snow and start fishing.

On another journey a 36-inch, eight-pound northern pike snatched my bait, which was a small perch, that I had caught earlier, the pike began to slowly move away with my little bait after taking about 50 feet of fishing line it stopped for roughly 10 seconds and then began to move once more at an accelerated rate. I instantly set the hook in its mouth and after a 20-minute battle the fish quit fighting, so I began to pull the fish toward a 12-inch diameter opening in the surface of the ice that was cut for us to fish from. As its head was coming up from the water with its mouth wide open showing many sharp menacing looking teeth, it barely made it through the 12-inch cavity in the ice. I was troubled when the fish was coming up to the surface of the ice and almost bit me. It seemed that it could have swallowed my hand and arm up to the elbow. If it had the opportunity with that thought in my mind, I nearly dropped it back in the water luckily my fishing partner Bill saved the day by keeping that from happening and saved the largest fish I ever caught from getting away.

With all these adventures, how can you not be hooked? If you had as much luck ice fishing as I had, I believe you would be hooked the same way I was.

Note to readers, the road to completing my story for this book has had several bumps, potholes and roadblocks of life. First of all, my son Michael died in October of 2018, in the Philippines.

Michael had gone there after meeting his future wife Antonina on the internet, with the intent of getting married to her. Soon after physically meeting her and her family he gave her an engagement ring, which he had bought at a jewelry store in downtown Chicago. After they were officially engaged and received her father's permission, they were married a month later. Their daughter is currently twelve years old.

Then on November 30th, 2018; I had a cardiac arrhythmia episode I was taken to Silver Cross's Hospital emergency room in New Lenox, Illinois by the New Lenox Fire Department paramedics. My symptoms included being light-headed, having cold sweats, nausea and minor chest pain; the doctor said it was from Broken Heart Syndrome. *(I never knew about what BHS was it is the diagnosis when a spouse dies and shortly afterwards the other spouse became severely distressed or depressed and/or also dies.) While in the ER my heart stopped. The doctor used a defibrillator to restart it. I woke up screaming and envisioned a mist floating from the ceiling, that looked like me enter my body. Subsequently, while I was hospitalized, I suffered a stroke on December 3rd from which I am still recovering. In mid-January, I was released from the hospital after receiving several weeks of excellent inpatient therapies. I then spent time at outpatient therapy where I also received excellent care.*

The latest roadblock, has been the loss of my grandson Shane who passed away at the end of March 2019.

Consequently, I needed help to finish the story, so with the

help of my daughter Jennifer to type the first draft. My writers'
family to help edit and offer suggestions to help finalize it for
publication. Plus, their encouragement as well as my wives and
other members of my family and friends who encouraged me not to
give up when the frustrations of life attempt to overwhelm me.

Getting Yourself Unstuck

by Awesome Angie Engstrom

I am crying and shaken to the core. Relieved that we have a diagnosis but frightened at the new path we must navigate as a family. I am amazed at how one hour in a behavioral optometrist's office can rock my world.

An hour ago, I didn't even know what a behavioral optometrist was.

***

Seasons come. Seasons go.

Have you ever looked at life in terms of seasons?

For instance, newlyweds navigate a season as they adjust to new life together. Couples becoming new parents is a season of change. Raising children has a variety of seasons within it.

Seasons of life bring change, and humans naturally resist change. Most seasons are somewhat expected and have typical weather patterns to them. However, each season also comes with occasional storms. Some of the storms bring dramatic and unexpected disruption to life's norm.

What happens when an unusual storm enters your life? How do you react, adjust, and cope in the face of atypical life circumstances?

103

What happens if you are already in a tough storm when another powerful storm moves in? One storm intersects with another and they join forces combining their energies. Then what do you do? Perhaps it seems like your forecast is always bringing more adversity to navigate. How do you cultivate the strength to keep moving through the storms of life verses getting flooded with the emotional turmoil?

The way I see it, if I'm progressing in some area of life and feel I'm in God's will, I'm at least on the right trajectory. When will this trajectory end?

It's been five long years since I dropped into a dark, internal storm.

Five long years of life have come and gone as I remain in this dark pit of numbness. I feel like I am in a parallel world. Life is moving on, but without me. I see the seasons of the planet changing. I see my son growing from an infant into a bubbly preschooler, yet I remain trapped in a pit of darkness as the world in all it's busy-ness keeps moving forward.

Little did I know that a new season of life had finally burst onto the horizon.

***

Life comes with storms, both literally and figuratively. Not all storms are in the forecast.

When storms of life happen and your horizon of hope transforms into dark uncertainty, how do you get yourself unstuck from the emotional surge hard-wired onto your humanity? How do you react, cope, and deal with circumstances beyond your control and move toward restoration and progress toward the life you desire?

Storms sometimes bring messes. I like the word, "mess" because messes can be cleaned up. Reframing circumstances to the positive magnifies a horizon of hope that allows me to see the possibilities rather than the obvious storm of adversity in front of me. This strategy was tested while raising our son. What follows is a brief overview of the season that tested and strengthened me and my family, as well as some of the lessons learned along the way.

Prior to this moment, my five-year-old son, Michael, was struggling socially due to random behavior issues that no medical professional could explain.

Michael was an extremely happy, alert, and spirited toddler: imaginative, energetic, and adventurous. He was a constant ball of motion, always keeping us on our toes. But as his mom, I knew something was special about Michael.

By the time he was eighteen months old, I had heard many comments from people about how active he was. Therefore, I asked the pediatrician to rate his level of activity. After cautiously searching for the right words, the doctor finally looked directly at me and said...

"You've got a livewire!"

What kind of diagnosis was that? Anyway, if the doctor

105

wasn't worried, why should I be?

In the controlled environment of our home, his behaviors were "normal." However, any time we were around other people, even family, he had unusual behavior outbursts that were loud, disruptive, and sometimes physical. As the mom, I felt the overwhelming blame – the mommy guilt – "Why can't I control my child's behavior?" I observed closely, looking for any pattern that triggered his outbursts, but no such pattern emerged. His unusual behaviors were completely random, yet the shame of this behavioral mess constantly overshadowed my spirit. Every incident magnified this perpetual season of uncertainty. Seeking peace amidst this storm became my daily survival tactic in order to keep my sanity.

Think of his behavior like a clock – tick-tock, tick-tock, tick-tock, CLUNK! Tick-tock, tick-tock, CLUNK! He seemed like a normal kid and then out of the blue, with no warning, and no way to predict, he would have a behavior outburst (the CLUNK!) so obnoxious that everyone would stop, look with amazement, and not know how to react. People would scatter as if saying, "Excuse us. We'll find other kids to play with." Social isolation became the new norm for our family.

Going anywhere in public, especially out to restaurants and shopping, were projects that needed strategic planning and a mental helmet to protect my sanity, as I learned to dodge judgmental stares.

Have you ever seen a mom trying to control a sensory-overloaded kid: loud, impulsive, can't sit still, and needs constant prompting to stay on task?

"Hello. Nice to meet you."

Preschool was the tipping point for me. The school would frequently call me to come pick up Michael early because he was so disruptive. On the days he did make it the whole two hours, it became the norm for all the other kids to run up to me like it was a competition to tell me all the bad things he did that day. My heart ripped open every day I had to endure the judgement, even from children. Picking him up from school was the lowest point of my daily existence.

Something was very wrong. The behaviors that the teachers and kids were describing were not anything that I had ever witnessed when he was in my care. It was as if they were describing a completely different kid.

With kindergarten around the corner, I knew we needed more time to figure out the best place for Michael socially and academically.

This is when I found myself in a behavioral optometry office.

Behavioral optometry is an expanded area of optometric practice that takes a holistic approach to eye and vision care, not just focal vision. I was introduced to new terminology such as: Ambient vision. Convergence insufficiency. Saccadic deficiency. Occupational therapy. Sensory processing disorder. Vestibular. Proprioception. All these new labels and terms.

What just happened to my world?

Did you know that a comprehensive eye assessment is recommended for infants during their first year of life? As a new mom, I wish I had known that. I was mistakenly led to believe that I could wait until school age to have Michael's eyes checked. Babies obviously can't read A, B, C and 1, 2, 3; so, what are the doctors looking for? If eye and vision issues are diagnosed and treated early enough, many problems can be avoided, including learning and permanent vision impairment. One in every ten children is at risk for undiagnosed eye and vision problems. Who knew, right? Check out www.InfantSEE.org if you know anyone under the age of one. That one tidbit of prevention could possibly save a family a lot of grief.

Anyway, this certainly was a messy season for our family, while at the same time a relief. We finally had a medical professional explain a hidden obstacle causing Michael's behavior issues after five years of observing, questioning, and coping the best we could.

After only fifteen minutes in her optometry chair, the doctor faxed a prescription to a rehabilitation hospital for an occupational therapy evaluation, put therapeutic glasses on my five-year-old son, and sent us out the door with pamphlets and homework.

Just four months earlier, we were at the pediatrician's office with a clean bill of health. Now, we were being sent to a rehabilitation hospital.

Talk about shock!

This news was an answer to our prayers for clarity, but the plan and path laid before us was a very costly one, on all levels, including financially, emotionally, and relationally.

Our family was at a crossroads. Is this the path to take? If so, how do we redesign our lives to make it happen?

Many questions and conversations occurred while navigating the proper, successful path to stability. All the individuals involved needed to agree with the plan in order to make consistent progress. Disagreements and resistance to new ideas slowed down the process.

The objections and excuses could have also taken over and kept us from moving forward. Here is a partial list:

- "That program is too expensive."
- "I'm not paying out of pocket for that treatment. If insurance doesn't cover it, forget it."
- "That's too far to drive. Too much time and gas money."
- "We need another opinion."
- "You know how much time I will have to take off work? We can't afford that."

Dwelling on the mess wasn't going to help anyone. Focusing on our family vision and creating a plan accordingly, despite the obvious obstacles, was essential. Without realizing it yet, making these hard decisions bridged their way into my parallel world of internal turmoil and I was coming alive again. My internal storm had been swallowed up by and even more fierce storm. By focusing on my son's new needs and off my internal turmoil, an undeserved favor lifted me out of the pit in order to advocate for Michael. There were many other excuses we could have made, but as a family, we allowed the big picture to drive our daily decisions.

As CEO's of the household, we defined everyone's roles. Mike took the financial burden, and I took the rest. I made the time to assemble the professional care team and drive the miles to get to everyone. My day became scheduled around our new priority: trusting this new treatment option for Michael.

Many miles, hours, and dollars later, the results of the treatments were slow and barely noticeable. So, the questioning continued: Are we doing the right thing? Do we choose other options presented to us? What other options do we have? Outside of the rehabilitation hospital, most of the people I talked to had never heard of sensory processing disorder (SPD). Others tried to give us labels that often overlap with SPD. The pediatrician was not on board, so we were carving a non-traditional path for Michael's treatments that was not covered by insurance. We tried just about every known modality we could afford that aligned with our vision.

Homeschooling became the optimal choice because his behaviors were triggered any time people were around. The larger the crowd, the bigger the disruption. Public school was not a favorable option.

Our family business had residual money coming in which allowed me to be a work-at-home mom, but it wasn't enough to support this phase of our life. As the pressures mounted from decisions that needed to be made despite the unknowns, and disagreements and discussions along the way, it was easy to see how families break apart, and often do, during these kinds of crises. Statistics show that families with kids that have extra-special needs have a much higher divorce rate. Just knowing that statistic helped me decide not to become one.

It got to a point to where our funds were almost gone.

The pressure was mounting, and my husband had had enough. "You are going to work and he's going to public school."

Yikes. My world had now completely shattered.

For Michael, enrolling him into a public-school situation knowing it was not the ideal environment for him, elevated my prayer status into high gear.

For me, going to work meant starting a business because that's what I knew how to do. What "job" was going to be flexible enough for our family's needs? If you can't find a way, make a way. Therefore, I created a business that worked within my schedule and gave me the flexibility I needed.

After entering public school, even with extra classroom assistance, Michael struggled and gradually became a very troubled and unhappy kid. That environment magnified his learning disabilities and crushed his self-confidence. Something is definitely wrong when your fourth grader exits the school building on a Friday afternoon and yells, "I'm done with this!" and intentionally runs into the path of a moving vehicle. I immediately contacted the school office to see what on earth happened that day; and they said, "Oh, he had a great day."

How can this be happening! Back to the not knowing.

Looking back on what I know now that parking lot incident was Michael's way of telling the world, "I do not feel safe, I am broken, and I don't fit in here." He couldn't put it into words then, but as he got older, he voiced how broken he felt.

Heartbreaking.

Before entering school, Michael was happily living life following the peace in his heart. Sometimes I call this the still, small voice. But upon entering school and getting more input from others with more worldly experience than him, he began to doubt, question, and ignore that peaceful whisper in his heart.

I was getting a lot of practice learning how to pay attention to the whispers in my heart that were gently urging me to make the tough decisions. However, to do that, I had to seek, with intentionality, the peace in my heart.

Peace became my new mentor.

Every decision seemed to come with an emotional charge. I was learning to stop feeding the voice that was trying to pull me down. I focused on feeding the voice that said, "take this path," or "make this choice," even when circumstances tried to steer me otherwise.

What do you mean, "follow peace?"

Think of it as a knowing in your heart. Perhaps it is a whisper you hear in your heart that is not coming from your thinking. We heard it as a child when we were naturally excited about life. But as we grew and received input from others who had more confidence and experience than us, those voices started crowding this peaceful whisper to where perhaps we could no longer hear it or even knew it existed in the first place.

When we retrain ourselves to follow peace, a whole new way of life unfolds. The peaceful whispers in my heart led me to let go of the outcome and trust the processes that the universe was providing.

After more advocating, Michael was transferred to a safer school environment.

At the same time, God led us to a fantastic program that ended up being the most intense. It incorporated every modality we were already doing independently, plus more into one customized program. If you know of a child that struggles with any kind of behavioral or learning issues, please consider taking the initial assessment at BrainBalanceCenters.com. For Michael, they found a new hidden obstacle: brain hemispheric imbalance.

However, this modality was the costliest of all the treatments we had ever considered. Do we make this investment in finances, time, and miles? This miraculous solution would not have presented itself if it wasn't meant for us. Our job was to step out in faith. We did, and it proved to be the missing piece we needed to assist Michael to the next level of stability.

I'm all about getting to the root of an issue so that the results are lasting. If you think like me at all, at the very least, invest in the evaluation portion; and then make a quality decision from the data they uncover for you.

***

This story only illustrates a fraction of the drama it took to help our son. I am happy to report that Michael is in a stable place; and it was worth every tear, tough conversation, and mile driven. We have our happy kid back and peace rules at the heart of our family. The past is done, the future is bright, and we find the joy in each moment with the experiential knowledge that wholeness always was, and always will be, with us when we live daily from this place of flow and ease. Every storm in life serves a purpose. When we stay determined to get through the storm and not stay stuck in the messy parts, the storm eventually transforms into something good.

During this behavioral storm, I was forced to completely take my eyes off my own internal storm. Interesting how without attention and energy, my internal storm of turmoil lifted. Storms can't exist if the environment is not optimal.

Storms come. Storms go. Over time, the seasons change too.

After years of sitting in waiting rooms, I met a lot of families. I love observing people. It was very clear to see the difference between the parents with a confident presence and peaceful demeanor, and those that couldn't find stable footing in their storm. This is what most people miss. If they cannot calm and center themselves, no matter the external circumstances, they are making decisions based on a rocky, unstable foundation verses creating from a sense of peace while they identify their priorities and make decisions.

When you find your peace, you find your power.

Seasons come. Seasons go.

Storms happen. Messes happen, and how we act and react to the messy seasons directly affects the outcome. We can choose our attitudes, our actions, and our association. Those daily choices make all the difference as we get ourselves unstuck and move toward the life we desire.

If we keep getting tripped up by our messes, it slows us down and can derail us from reaching the target. Some people don't even know their target. And if you are in a pit of darkness, never stop watching for that season to change. Be deliberate about the life you want to create. Vision creates the energy that you need to take the next step. Allow that energy to drive you through the messy season toward creating the newest version of the masterpiece of your life.

I encourage you to cast a clear vision for your family based on your values, create a plan, and be accountable to the small, daily actions of that plan as you follow peace along the way. Know that the seasons will change, and storms will come. Know that new energy and new circumstances come with those changes. It's your attitude, your preparedness, and your willingness to accept the new path that makes a world of difference. Allow your family vision to guide each decision. When the plan gets challenged, and it will, decide to live moment by moment by following the small whispers in your heart.

115

When life gets messy, how do you pick up the pieces and craft the next layer of your masterpiece called life, while keeping your sanity intact? How do you get yourself unstuck from the messes of life and transition into the new season?

Looking back, I see how this experience has strengthened me for my mission in life. I now coach families and small business owners on how to focus their time to achieve more in their day, while making plenty of time for their family's needs.

There is greatness inside you. You will either impact this world in a positive way or allow the external circumstances of life to keep you down. Don't leave it up to chance. Choose a life of peace despite the circumstances and make an impact on others that will last beyond your lifetime. It's up to you to stay in charge of your daily attitudes and decisions, and it's worth every effort necessary to move toward this new lifestyle of living.

The power is in you. Life is too precious to waste another moment being stuck. Break through your obstacles, create the processes and systems you need, and move with intention toward the life you want. Never allow the storms of life derail you.

FOLLOW PEACE

Quivering Up to Old Age

by Carolyn Hill

Ah... yes my dear Judy, the warmth of this night's fireside burns quick, crackles, and hisses without warning. So does the warmth of the heart and the bitter cold moments of our lives. How low I feel... Some days the restlessness and uncertainty of my twilight years hover softly. Winter's shadow clouds my memory.

Yet, I manage to remember. Oh, how I remember back to when it began. A very long aisle carpeted in heavenly blue and what I thought was an angel floating my way. Even then, as nervous as I was, I believed the two of us would discover the secret of staying young and quivering right up to old age.

In our special place, I sit in quiet reflection with only a vision of the girl I married. Your infectious smile burns into my old soul more than ever. When I look, I see a girl standing in front of me, shy with twinkling eyes that flirt just for me. Though your chestnut hair is cast with the white snow of age, you have managed to bring the summer into the shadows of my heart when I least expected it. The blush of innocence is now long gone. But, no matter my dear... To me you are the light of my existence. I shall forever love you.

Loneliness taunts me, as my thoughts replay day in and day out. Oh, the struggles of youthful disillusion. How many times you loved, and let me be me. I didn't say it often enough, but you permeated my manly soul and touched the wanton heart of this fool. Somehow you knew what I wanted before I did.

Sweetheart, you turned my cold world upside down the first time we touched body to soul. I remember the kiss in your eyes as I pulled you slowly into my arms. I could feel the warmth and flush of your skin against my cheek. The air lingered with the arousing scent of your perfume and my heart began to race. All the other sounds of the world silenced. Our first kiss ... kissed my soul, and I knew. You were the one!

Now only a ghostly love remains. I struggle and live with half a love changed by the undertow of life's fickle seasons. The tingling excitement is gone from within the four walls of this place we called our home. I'm lost... No longer is there the wonderful rush of our youth evident, or the trials of our middle years which threatened to tear us apart. Even what might have been in our senior years, shrinks slowly into oblivion as I grapple for any precious memory left of our Love.

Somehow time withered away into seasons neither one of us dreamed would pass so quick. Here I sit paralyzed in its grasp hoping for something, anything to stop the agony flooding my aching heart. Each day the memories of our love seems to deepen my pain, and I can't seem to emerge out of its darkness, and I wonder...

Would I do it all over again? You betcha! Judy girl, right now, I'd even settle for a good old fashion fight. Then for sure, you and I would start again quivering up to old age.

118

Spring in Yellowstone

by Diane Perry

In the early morning the red-glowing sun is rising above the snow-covered mountaintops. Seven thousand feet high, we drive following the road that curves left, then back to the right. All of a sudden, taillights of campers, recreational vehicles and cars are seen, there is a backup for fifty feet. Bear Jam! Curious, scanning the area with our eyes, a large black bear and her cub are running freely on the side of the mountain crossing the road in front of the jam. They continue to run through the melting snow and down to the river for a drink of fresh water. Enthusiastically, the people in their vehicles are hanging out the open windows taking a snapshot of the beautiful sight.

After their hibernation, the bears are running and playing exuberantly.

"I guess the paparazzi are intrigued by my baby, Lulu. Before I fell asleep for the winter, I became pregnant. My hibernation continued for months until I woke up and saw Lulu for the first time. She is my joy and I will take care of her for two or three years until I feel she can be left by herself," says Mama Bear. "I am so happy I ate enough huckleberries and plants beforehand to nourish Lulu because I literally did not eat or drink for three months."

After the traffic clears, we are on the road again to reach Old Faithful which is in the Southern end of the National Park. To our right cars are parked neatly near the valley to get a look at the

119

bison lying near a creek with geysers around smoldering from volcanic heat. The tourists are gathering to set up their tripod cameras for the bison since they are one-hundred-twenty feet away.

"Oh, I am so happy they are taking pictures of my two calves," says Mama Bison. "Twins are a rarity for us, and quite a handful so they are protected not only by me, but by the rest of the herd. Since my duty is to wean them for seven to thirteen months, I sent Papa to the other side of the valley as now he is referred to as a 'bachelor'. He is constantly rubbing himself against a tree to peel off all his matted winter fur."

Meanwhile, after packing up our field scope, and setting forth for a new destination being Hayden Valley which is the home of the wolf. Mother wolf is usually in her den with her new pups at this time. However, there is a frenzy of cars in front of us again. This time the backup goes for a full mile because there is a sight of a wolf in the valley.

"I will stay with my pups in the nursery for eight weeks until they come out of the den for the first time. My litter can be four to five pups, but I only have three this time," says Mother Wolf. "Dad is outside pacing for our protection. He is a most fascinating father because of his loyal partnership to me for life."

Our day is coming to an end as we approach our cabin in Mammoth Hot Springs for the night. It is dusk and there are many, many elk with their baby calves bopping around as if they are on pogo sticks. After the calves have grazed in the field, they are thirsty and poke Mama Elk for the milk to be nursed. As we come around the corner of our cabin to get a snapshot of this delightful sight, mother elk has her head just above the grass line to keep an eye on us.

"I am protecting my young and will charge these spectators if I feel they are too close. A recommendation is to stay at least twenty-five feet away from all of us," says Mother Elk. "Along with the other mothers, I need to keep babies close to me for six months."

The elk bucks are in the forest at this time shedding their antlers due to low testosterone levels making the bone brittle. In early spring, March or April, their antlers sprout up and are covered with velvet, then they become strong with keratin growing four feet above their heads. Surprisingly, new ones grow every late spring which are used for fighting another buck for the female during mating season which is in autumn. You will hear a "cluck, cluck, cluck" when they are in a match.

Yellowstone National Park spans the states of Idaho, Montana, and Wyoming. It doesn't get warmer than mid-eighty degrees in the summer months. It is a scenic park to see nature at its best. We hope to visit this beautiful, peaceful place again sometime.

Please note these facts were given by the Park Rangers when visiting the Education Centers in throughout park.

Life's Seasons

by Jolee L. Price

My life began in a hospital that no longer exists except in my mother's memories. Seven years later, my sister was born, and that hospital still exists and operates to this day.

A lot of my childhood years were visits with my father's mother. Sundays were the traditional family supper day. She always gave us homemade chicken soup to take home in a small white enamel pot which my mom gave to me, and I still have to this day. I also spent time at her home during the summer. We had a special bond. She was of Hungarian descent and spoke only in Hungarian even though she knew English. Of course, being an immigrant, learning English was required to becoming an American Citizen. I think she wanted me to learn her language, so we could have some sort of connection with her ethnicity. I did okay with the language, but when she passed in 1972, so did most of the knowledge of what I had learned. Sadly, my father passed away in 2013.

Until my sister was born, the kids on our block were boys, and I quickly became a tomboy. Riding and racing our bikes, playing catch and baseball were the norm. I was quite the bike racer. These games did not last because soon the boys were gone, and families with girls moved in. I went from playing baseball to playing with Barbies. I also became a Brownie and advanced to a

Girl Scout. The cookies were a deal breaker.

Because of the seven-year age difference, our family doctor mentioned to my mom to involve me with my sister to help alleviate rivalry, mainly because newborns take a lot of time, care, and attention. One of the involvements was to help change my sister's diapers. Back then, diapers were cloth and baby safety pins were used. Some of the plastic tops on the pins were faces of yellow ducks. Non-shaped tops were in colors of pink and blue. I wanted to do a good job; however, I have to say that I could neither eat nor stand the sight of yellow mustard for years.

At first, it was mainly fun, but as I got older, the years between us seemed more than seven. When I became fourteen, my sister was seven. I was a teenager. She was a child. When I became a woman, she was a teenager.

It's funny about age. We had the innocence of fun and games in the early years. We had the awkwardness of growing pains in the middle years. We now have a connection that grows with experience and maturity in our later years. Emotions of anger and happiness wavered, and still do at times, but love never did. It's ironic the age gap of seven years has dissipated. I know it's there, but it doesn't feel like it to me at this stage of our lives.

My active imagination was always getting me into trouble, in one way or another, in grammar school. To me, the classroom was the stage, and my classmates were the audience. If they could or would not talk to me, I would talk to them, the walls or the ceilings. I even talked to the air or whatever was in front of or near me. It did not matter. I was not choosey. I even answered myself. Unfortunately, my conversations and animated theatrics were usually during class time. Though helpful later in school plays, in class, the teacher was the disciplinarian.

I was disciplined many times. My mother was always getting notes about my talking in class. I truly believe my mother's hair started going gray when I was six years old. My mom told me as a baby I had colic for six months. From my point of view, I was a communicator from birth. Ah, but that was then. Going from trying to be front and center to being on the side lines is comforting.

Being a little girl, I remember wanting to be like my mother by getting married at eighteen like she did. However, when I became eighteen, I said to myself, "yeah, right!" I then surmised I would marry by the age of twenty-one or never. I did get married at twenty-seven and still am, thirty-four years later.

My skills of typing and shorthand were learned in high school.

I went to a Catholic high school. I have my mother to thank for these classes. For my Junior year, I signed up for Cooking and Sewing. Unbeknownst to me, when my mother took me to pick up my class schedule and books, Shorthand 1 and Typing 1 were listed. I immediately showed her the school's mistake on my schedule. She said there was no mistake and told me she had called the school demanding my schedule be changed shortly after I told her of my class picks. This was a "tough love" moment of my mother's choosing. She said it was for my own good, and that I would thank

124

her one day. I later admitted (many years later) that she chose well. I possess these class skills to this day, although my shorthand speed has diminished. I continue to use shorthand and still have the uncanny habit of taking a telephone message for my husband in shorthand. I've gotten much better at translating messages for him. I still have my pins I won for shorthand and typing tests. I graduated in the Bicentennial year of 1976. By the way, as for cooking, I'm a good cook. As for sewing, I can sew a button. Mom was right.

Disco was where it was at when I obtained legal drinking age.

I remember buying my first pair of genuine disco shoes with the five-inch acrylic heels from an Aldens catalog. I endured much laughter, including from myself as I practiced walking in them while holding on to the walls for balance. I felt like Bambi in the scene where he tried to walk on the ice, and his legs kept going out from underneath him. It took me a week of daily practice, but my perseverance paid off, and I was disco-dancing with my girlfriends. I continue to love dancing to this day, and yes, I still have those disco shoes. Sentimentality has kept me from tossing them away. My shoes now consist of pumps, flats and tennies. It's funny how practicality plays a major hand in the course of aging. I heard it said that "we all age, just don't get old." To me, this means live and enjoy life in moderation; don't exist.

I worked for lawyers for many years. I must admit that I was blessed with the lawyers I had worked for. I know the work load they hold, and the commitment required. That hold and commitment can take a toll on a marriage and/or family.

Working in the City of Chicago was a love of mine. There is nothing like the rush you feel when you are in the city. The hustle and bustle are a natural adrenaline high. Then one morning I stared out of the train window wondering if this was all there was. As I was watching the scenery flash by, I was reminded that was how my life was going – same scenario, different day. There had to be more to life than the same-old monotony of twelve to fourteen-hour days. I realized my life was consumed by my job with a huge part being travel time, which was a three-hour round trip. This left me little time to do anything else or get anything done in the workday evenings. Back then, banks, dry cleaners and even butcher shops were usually closed by 6:00 P.M. Weekends were filled with errands and housework.

By later joining a law firm in Joliet, my travel time was approximately twenty minutes compared to an hour and a half one way. The savings of my travel time was exciting; however, I didn't know how to handle all this extra time at first. I became anxious at wondering what to do with my time. This anxiety did not last long. Slowly but surely, family and friends were reentering my life. While working at the Joliet firm lacked the "city adrenaline rush" of Chicago, it more than made up for it in its local charm. The firm in Joliet was small, quaint and extremely family oriented. It had its own style. I have remained friends with some of my former co-workers due to that atmosphere.

126

I knew my husband for some time before we started dating. We were friends, and I believe our friendship was an integral part of our relationship. One thing I learned is that the word "compromise" plays a major role in relationships. If it works while you dated, it should work when you say, "I do" or in my case, "I will." Compromise can lay and plant a good groundwork in building a foundation of sacrifice and sharing while weeding out selfishness and self-centeredness.

This takes time. Psalm 37:34 states "I won't be impatient for the Lord to act! I will keep traveling steadily along His pathway and in due season (seed, time, harvest) He will honor me with every blessing." [emphasis mine] God's ways are not man's ways. His timetable is not ours. Impatience is neither godly nor healthy.

We soon married and were in the next season of our lives in the formidable circle of life. The stereotypical blueprint for life is grow up, get a job, get married, get a home, have children and retire. Well, we grew up, had jobs, got married, bought a home but the children never came although my husband has two beautiful daughters from a prior marriage. Adoption was briefly discussed but never followed up. The pain of not having a child is brutal. I still have our baby hope chest packed away, filled with items I thought we would need. I did have a false-positive result once to a pregnancy test. I still remember my hopeful anticipation of the results. My husband even bought a bottle of champagne. A "yes" from the doctor would be a small sip. A sip didn't happen. A hopeful answer and champagne both went down the drain.

Years later, my husband retired, and I quit sometime after to become a housewife. Church is important to us. We are Christians and God, the triune, is an integral part of our lives.

My husband, I and our dogs love to take trips in our camper. Our lives are simple. We are never bored, and I have more than made up for those three hours in travel time I gave up years ago. I love the simpler times of life that are hardly noticed in the ongoing fast pace of life also known as the rat race. While I do at times miss the old "Chicago Loop" days, I do not miss the frantic pace and truly relish the slower stride of my life now.

One morning as the sunlight filtered in through the blinds, birds were chirping away. I thought this was simplicity at one of its best. The singing birds were not the Philharmonic Orchestra, but they were and are just as melodious. The birds have a patent on simplicity for living. They prove this every season. They live and move on. They are living proof of the circle of life. Instead of begrudging a monotonous life, season in and season out, they live. They do not exist, and I could not agree more.

We Went Camping

by Sylvester Kapocius

C amping was fun. We'd get away from daily chores and the same ole environment. It was a relief. I first thought of camping at ten.

In 1938, Eddie, the only boy from our neighborhood, was in the Boy Scouts. His folks could afford those fees. With that group, he camped often and told us stories.

My neighbor, BZ, asked my brother, Ben, and I if we cared to go camping and fishing at the Momence River. That excited us so much. He said, Go ask your dad if you can."

When we asked our dad, the answer was a flat no. We pleaded for permission, and he almost caved in. HE said, "Call BZ over so I can talk with him."

They talked for a while, then my dad told BZ, "Okay, but just remember, you're responsible for my two boys."

BZ was a bachelor of thirty. He did not realize his responsibility over us. BZ's older friend came with us. The four of us took off in BZ's rattletrap car.

When we left that Friday, the sky was clear and bright, just before sundown. The journey seemed long. An hour's ride got us there, in the dark.

All we brought for shelter was a tarpaulin. We used long,

dead tree branches to support the tarp. We attached the poles to metal stakes in the ground with ropes.

No sooner was that done than rain poured and poured, almost all night long. My brother Ben and I sat in the car for hours. BZ and his friend sat under the tarp and sipped whiskey from their half-pint bottle.

We never told our dad about that.

It finally stopped raining about 3 a.m. The river rose and the current was rapid. At five, the water flowed slower, and Ben did not wait any longer to start fishing. He baited his hook with a worm, and as soon as he lowered his pole and the hook sank in the water, he snagged a half-pound white bass. When he raised the pole, the fish fell off and into the water. He jumped off the bank instantly, three feet down to the fast-flowing water and grabbed the fish. He angrily said, "It ain't gonna get away from me." It scared me when he jumped in the river. I bawled him out because he was not a good swimmer.

Our fishing luck was good. We caught seven white bass. With the dry wood we brought from home, a fire was started under the small grill. We fried the fish and shared some with BZ and his friend.

It soon became hot and humid, so we packed up and headed for home. As we rode, we talked about having a better camping trip next time.

When we returned home, our mom greeted us with a smile

and said, "I did not sleep too well while you were gone."

In 1952, I drove to California to visit some Navy buddies. On my way home from there, I visited the Ponderosa House at Lake Tahoe, Nevada. The campground close by was jampacked with tents and recreational vehicles. What remained in my mind after I saw what was there, camping was cheaper than taking a room in a motel. I thought, *that's the way to go.*

Ten years went by. We were a family of five. It was vacation time, but my pocketbook was crunched. I thought of camping and said, "That's the way to go." Our auto was in good shape so with my wife and three children, we agreed to start the adventure of camping.

We decided to camp on sites that surrounded Lake Michigan for a start. I purchased a tent, five sleeping bags, and five folding stools. A relative donated a small cooking stove and I had an old kerosene lantern to use in the tent at night. That Saturday morning, we started out with the baggage strapped on the car's roof, and the rest went in the trunk.

We began from our house in Chicago. I drove around the south bend of the lake to New Buffalo, Michigan, which was our first choice. We all pitched in and fumbled around setting up the tent. After getting organized, we walked around the entire camp, had a snack, and fell asleep in the tent.

In the wee hours of the morning as the sun rose, our four-year-old son Keith popped his head up repeatedly and looked around. It was too early to get up. I told him to go back to sleep several times, but he just continued to get up.

Then we sat up together and I asked him, "What's your problem?"

He answered, "Somebody turned the tent around."

"What?" I exclaimed.

I brought him out of the tent and showed him the tent was in the same position as the previous night. Well, after going through a slightly difficult discussion with him, he said, "When we left home, the lake was on this side," while pointing to the east. "When I awoke, the lake was on that side," and he pointed to the west. I immediately pulled out a map and showed him the road we took around the south end of the lake. Then he saw why the lake was seen from the other side of the tent. He understood what I explained to him, and from that time on he became interested in maps.

In the morning we had an awkward time at breakfast. No hot meal, only juice and cold cereal with milk. My wife, Betty, was happy, just a few bowls to wash.

It was a little cool that morning as we toured around the entire area. We rested and visited other campers. The kids made friends in a very short time.

Our next stop was Grand Haven, Michigan. When I pulled into the gas station there in July, a six-foot-high pile of snow from the winter remained on the edge of the station's lot. The owner said they had a very heavy snowfall during the past winter. We gassed up and drove north to find our next campsite.

It was time for lunch. We found a restaurant, ate there, and were satisfied with the food and service.

When the waitress handed me the bill, on the reverse side it had a phone number scribbled on it. I showed it to Betty and I said, "Folks must have been really lonely around this place in the winter."

That became more evident as we traveled north.

Our next stop was Ludington. We set up camp in a state park on nice green grass, away from the lake. We hiked and played all day. It became cool in the evening as the temperature dropped, which was unusual for July. I shivered that night. At six in the morning, I got up, grabbed a can of warm beer from a six-pack, and drank it while I sat on a stool outside of the tent. The sun rose slowly over the high treetops from the east, which warmed me a bit.

Keith awoke soon after me, and as soon as he unzipped the tent, six tiny frogs, one after another, jumped from the frosted grass and into the tent. Mom gave him a small jar to keep them in.

At our next stop we filled up with gas, and we needed ice for the cooler. Nobody was seen inside or outside the station, so I asked the owner if he had some for sale. He said, "Some and follow me with your car to my garage." That sort of bothered me, but I did what he said.

Inside the garage were large sheets of plywood which covered a thick canvas blanket over ice blocks in the ground. He chopped a block of ice for our cooler and covered that huge pile of ice. He said their winter job was to cut ice blocks out from the lake and store them in the garage for summer sales.

I paid him for the ice and then he noticed Keith's frogs in the jar. He said, "They are good fish bait. I'll give you a quarter for them."

Keith's face beamed a bit and he said okay and sold his frogs to him.

A whole week had passed, and we headed for the Fisherman's Island, south of Charlevoix. At the campsite, we played ball, hiked a while, and saw a sign that read, "Tour the Nuclear Reactor Site in Charlevoix."

I thought it would be interesting, so we all went. About fifteen people attended. We clipped film badges on our clothing that monitored radioactivity.

The guide took up directly up to the control room. The operator at the console said the reactor was shut down and not in operation because the spent uranium fuel was being replaced with new fuel. He lectured us on the entire operation of the facility, but only a few in attendance seemed interested.

The following day, we moved to our next campsite. I drove over the Mackinac Bridge, but we did not visit the island. We had little time left with our vacation. I didn't find any campsites until we got to the other side of the lake. A sign on the highway showed camping ahead on a small lake around Manistee. We found it and it was a very enjoyable place where we swam and camped.

At night I saw a pile of evergreen branches at the dump site, so I used them to build a small bonfire in the open area of the camp. Everyone enjoyed the nice, bright, hot fire. Then the fire got slightly out of hand as the sparks flew through the trees behind camp. It was so hot from its own combustion that the sparks and flames swirled up high over the trees. I became worried. After twenty minutes, the fire burned down and I was relieved.

Two days were left to get home. I drove straight to the Chain of Lakes state park campground in Illinois. We explored the park for some possible future camping. Many campers filled that park, boaters galore on the lake.

We got home on Sunday, and I shot right over to KFC and brought home chicken for our dinner. When we were camping, we only ate two meals a day and snacked in between.

***

Camping was a simple way for me to enjoy life, and it was also exciting to explore new territory away from the city's hustle and bustle. Outdoor recreation had always been my activity zone. I dreaded the thought of being a couch potato.

After that first camping trip around Lake Michigan, I was ready to go camping again. This time it was at the state park in Kankakee, Illinois.

At that place, much of the land was barren and muddy. Puddles remained everywhere for days. Very few spaces with grass were available to set up the tent, and they were occupied when we arrived.

Later, a new campground was carved out in the weeds away from the water. The new area contained three campsites, two with electric hookups.

We used the rough camping site, which was furthest from the entrance. I brought firewood from home to cook with, and some more to burn during evening fireside chats. We camped there often when visiting family members and friends who lived in the Chicago suburbs while we lived in Missouri.

After evening meals, we walked the paths through the entire three camps. As we walked, we met folks with different lifestyles. We silently mocked the ones that brought the entire city's conveniences with them instead of enjoying outdoor living.

One place we camped at had cloggers who entertained us. Another time, a group of country-western musicians played for us. They were all really good. Another time, a someone demonstrated some home appliances for sale and dished out food samples. At camps near the water, boaters offered ride. A few places had horseshoe pits.

Camping in Marseilles, Illinois, was fun. There barges passed on the river and moved right by our camp. Each time one went by, the barge crew and pilot waved to us.

One night as we camped there, I heard a horn from a distance. It was a train of barges approaching. Being surrounded by woods, nothing was visible, but the toot of the horn was heard. Minutes later it was louder while coming down the river toward us.

I said to those around our campfire, "I will have you meet the pilot of the barge train as it goes by; just watch."

The lead barge, the first of five loaded units, came into sight

137

with its huge, bright, arc-type spotlight beaming ahead brightly over the center of the river. As soon as the tugboat pushing from the rear came into sight, I signaled with my flashlight, waving it slowly up and down while pointing it at the pilot house. The keen eyes of that pilot caught my signal immediately.

He turned his thirty-inch spotlight away from the river and shined it directly at me, which lit up the entire camp bright as daylight, while at the same time he blew his loud-as-ever horn. It made me feel like his entire humongous barge train was going to plow right through our camp. It scared a lot of people, but passed by in a very short time.

I knew it was a good show because everyone in camp raved about it.

Years later, we ran up and down that river with our first boat. I remember the first time, I lowered my boat off the ramp and into the water. Some boaters knew it was my first time.

One warned me, "Never cross the river in front of a moving barge." He said, "One did. His boat's power conked out as he crossed. He and his boat got swamped beneath the hull of the lead barge and completely disappeared."

It takes about two long city blocks for a barge to come to a complete stop.

I changed my ideas on how to improve our camping methods. The box I built to carry equipment on the roof of the car was a bit troublesome to load and unload. I did all of it myself. So I figured that on our following trips, things had to be different and better.

I bought a smaller car to save on gas. Then I built a small, one-wheeled trailer. The most expensive part of the trailer was the tire. It cost twice the price of a wheelbarrow tire, though both were the same size. It supported over one-hundred pounds, and it absorbed shocks from highway bumps at speeds up to eighty miles an hour, though our car only went sixty.

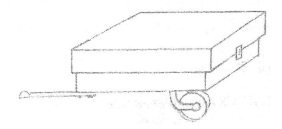

We had all winter to plan our summer vacation. We planned to camp for three weeks away from home. We chose to go far south. The list for the trip was long, and the day of the vacation came soon.

I loaded the trailer with all the necessary camping equipment. In the trunk we stored clothing, highway deflectors, and six long-burn flares for highway emergencies.

We wanted to see how camping was down south. We camped in Kentucky – oh, those gorgeous orange-and-purple-colored blossoms on those mimosa tree that grew on that bright bluish-green grass along the highway. Then we drove across the state line into Louisiana and found a place to set up camp in the national forest.

It was late afternoon and the tent went up very quickly. I dug a very narrow ditch, about two inches wide in the dirt, around the entire tent and poured used motor oil in the ditch. I was concerned about snakes entering the tent from the forest's scrabbly terrain. After a late dinner, we went to sleep.

At about eleven o'clock I heard voices. I peeked outside and saw two other campers had loaded and left. We were all alone in the woods. Then I observed and realized there was no authority or security around anywhere. It got scary.

I went back into the tent and laid back on my mattress to sleep. I reached under my pillow to check if my homemade Billy club was there.

Right after midnight, voices woke me. I peeked through an opening of the tent and saw four young adult men hullabaloo-ing with gusto. They all drank moonshine from the same jug.

We were disturbed by their noises and could not sleep. Then I heard a couple of stones bounce against our tent. After that, I heard stones bounce off the trees all around us. We could not sleep. No one else was in these woods except those drunken ones and us. I dared not approach then to ask for quiet. They sang, danced and drank until about 5 a.m. All of the sudden, a noisy vehicle started up and they left. I hoped to see their faces to report to some authority, but even that might have been useless.

After a quick breakfast, we packed up and drove back north, right over the Arkansas state line.

Folks at the gas station suggested that we should eat at the nice family restaurant down the street. There we had a catfish dinner that was quite outstanding. I was prepared in the Cajun style of cooking. They also suggested we camp at the Devil's Den Campground. They said it was real different and that we would like it, so I drove to it.

The roads to get there had sharp curves and they continued that way downhill for miles.

When we arrived there and entered the camping area, it felt like I drove in the basement of the Earth. Our voices bounced from the hills around us. If someone talked louder than a whisper, it was heard across the entire campground.

A cement pond was right in the middle of camp. I liked that and so did everyone else. We played in the water too hard, became tired, and fell asleep before ten.

At seven the next morning, I heard cows mooing outside the tent. When I opened the flap, one was close enough to walk in. I herd of seven tromped right through the center of camp. Nobody guided them as they traveled down the road and out of sight.

Just before lunch, thunderclouds burst right above us and rumbled as loud as a battleship's big guns. It scared everyone. Hail as large as baseballs fell and bounced on the tin roof of the washroom. It sounded like beating drums.

As you would know it, Cindy had to go to the washroom badly right then. The building was far away. We were prepared for such emergencies. In the tent, we draped a plastic bag over a metal bucket, and all went well.

The minute the hailstorm ended, a six-inch-high pile of snowballs were on the ground. I checked to see if the windshield of my car was cracked. It was not, but five slight dents showed on the trunk. It became hot and humid when the sun appeared again. Everything on the ground melted in thirty minutes.

That Saturday, a man came through the camp and announced for all in camp to attend a hillbilly wedding reception that evening. I asked him where. He said, "Right here in camp at six o'clock. All campers are invited." I looked around and counted twenty-five people.

Sure enough, right on time, the bride and groom appeared in wedding garb.

Everyone congratulated them. Then the groom picked up his bride and slung her right into the swimming pool, clothes and all. She stayed wet for a while then entered the trailer and changed to a bathing suit. She saw her husband was busy rambling with friends at the edge of the pool. That was her opportunity to get even. She shoved him over the edge of the pool and into the water. Everyone cheered loud as ever while he climbed out soaking wet and hugged her with a kiss.

142

Cake and coffee were served as we chatted for hours. It brought us strangers all together as one happy family. I will never forget it.

I learned a lesson or two each time I camped. When we watched the kids do their own thing, it was entertaining. Playing out in the fresh air was good for them as well as for us.

Keith was a very curious child. He was our best little camper. He scrounged up sticks and wood for every fire for cooking and snacking at night. At the age of twelve, he wielded a hatchet like a pro.

Once he walked over to investigate a rotted tree stump. HE poked it with a stick and inside was a hornet's nest. They awoke and attacked him. He got stuck on his forehead in two places at once. He cried and cried. Then the stins puffed his eyebrows so large, skin bulged over his eyes. After an hour, the swelling decreased and the pain left. That allowed him to see again.

When we camped near water, we fished. If bait was hard to come by, our two boys seined for minnows.

Catfish were my favorite, the one-and-a-half pounder. I roasted a potato to eat with it. With a little butter and salt in it, it was a great meal.

At the Pokagen State Park in Indiana, three young girls dared each other to jump over hot charcoal embers on the ground with their bare feet. One stumbled and both her feet landed on those smoking charcoals.

An out-of-town doctor who camped two sites away observed the incident and came to her aid. He offered the girl's mother some medication and said, "You may use this on her burned feet, but I cannot practice medicine in this state."

The next day passed quickly, and soon after dinner we walked throughout the entire campground as usual. We met more folks with different jokes and some had many stories to tell.

I was surprised that so many folks who camped with us were from such faraway places. A retired firefighter with his wife from Monticello, Indiana, stayed away from home for a year as they traveled around the country in a house on wheels.

At certain times we leaned on each other for information or assistance. Very few places had services or products to sell. Some campers were very experienced. At times we could not handle some situations by ourselves, therefore, we learned from their advice.

We saved specifically for our vacation. One year it was a trip to the Wisconsin Dells. It cost a lot to rent a cabin on stay at a motel, which would subtract from some entertainment on the trip, so I inquired at the tourist information booth in the Dells for a campsite nearby. Rather than answering, they flung brochures over the counter at me that advertised only cabins and motels. Finally, one young lady helped me. She said, "Rocky Arbor Park is a bit far, but straight down the highway only a few minutes' drive." That was great. We headed right to it. I paid five bucks for use of a campsite.

Huge, tall pine trees lined the blacktop road through the entire area as I drove. Because the trees were so high and so close together, the sun was blocked out by 4 p.m. It seemed like a short day. I drove around and found an empty site. We set up our tent and unloaded our baggage. Then I drove to the business section in town where most of the activity took place.

We took a ride on the Amphibious Duck. It was a bit thrilling, even though it rattled noisily as it moved slowly on the water.

By 10 p.m., we'd had it. We returned to the campground and got lost inside. It was so dark. No lights or moonlight. No street signs anywhere. Every direction looked alike, this way and that way. I drove in circles. I was lost. Cindy, who was only nine, kept repeating to me, "Dad, go this way." I just ignored her. Then I finally listened to her and found the way to our campsite. Cindy, our little guiding angel.

We were attacked by lots of mosquitoes that night, and some snuck into our tent. They did not want to leave.

We were fortunate to have four days of beautiful weather while we camped in the Wisconsin Dells area. However, we did not sit in camp all day.

The professional Tommy Bartlett ski team was advertised all over, but it was in Baraboo, on Lake Delavon, ten miles south. We attended that show and really liked it. They all performed like clockwork. They jumped simultaneously over the ramps floating on the water. The water needed to be very calm to perform that act, and it was that day.

Since that time, 1956, I saw performances by the same name, give their act in Missouri, and another time during 2014, at Black River Falls, Wisconsin.

On the lake there, girls in red, white, and blue costumes

performed on water skis standing three high on each other's shoulders. What a fabulous performance that was. Wow!

***

This was our typical camping set-up.

Easy to put up, easy to take down.

With two people, it took no time at all. That tent stood up through heavy winds and rain. The very effective way we staked it in the ground made rain flow off of it quickly, and as the wind arched it back and forth, that tent resisted gales of up to fifty miles per hour, which we endured at least twice during our entire camping years. It never collapsed.

Some places made it convenient for campers to cook and boil water to wash dishes and wash clothes, such as this one:

147

At some places we camped, observers came out from the woods like this one, as if saying, "You're encroaching on our property."

One time we invited friends to camp with us. They came with their canvas-top trailer. They feared being far from other campers and deep in the woods. I kept that in mind.

That night, after midnight, I tied a piece of meat to the tassel of their camper top. In twenty minutes, a raccoon came and struggled to loosen that food from their camper top. That awoke everyone inside. A lot of commotion erupted with loud voices and concern.

In the morning they could not wait to tell us of all the excitement which caused them some loss of sleep.

Betty and I had a hard time keeping from laughing.

The kids played wherever they found pleasure. Not once have I heard one of them say, "I don't have anything to do."

We always kept a third eye on them – you know, kids will be kids.

Jim, Cindy and Keith surely grew up fast. They began camping on their own, before and after having families. Now their children are campers. What copycats.

One couple that camped with us said, "We will bring steaks for all of us next time." Wow, great.

We camped right at the edge of the woods in the shade. It was nearly sundown and time to cook the steaks. The table to eat on was only ten feet from the thick brush leading into the woods. The cooler which contained the food was about ten feet from the table. I picked two steaks out of the cooler and placed them on the table. When I turned around to take more from the cooler, a large raccoon near the cooler faced me with one our steaks in its mouth. It ran into the woods with it.

I bolted right toward it. The raccoon stopped to look back at me. As he did that, I jerked the steak right out of its mouth. It stared at me for a second then took off into the woods.

I felt a bit uneasy after pulling that stunt.

I think that raccoon watched us eat those steaks with envy while hiding somewhere in the brush.

Each place we camped at was significant in my mind. Some were very unusual events and most entertaining. One of those situations still stands out in my mind. It took some of the local talent to plan, construct, and make it good enough to attract the general public.

My friend Perry from Leasville, South Carolina, told me about one of those events that took place in his area. I did not understand the situation as he described it to me until I ran across one of those actual events. The whole show was centered around hunters' hunting dogs. I would name it, *The Raccoon Chase.*

The animal – I believe it was a raccoon – was released from its cage into one end of a ditch filled with water. Dogs were released to chase after it. The hunting dogs swam after it, paddling as vigorously as ever, barking loudly along the way. Water splashed down the trail, but before the raccoon was caught, it was retrieved from the water safely at the end of the ditch.

The dog that led the parade to the finish put a great big smile on its owner's face. Some betting took place within the crowd.

You win some, you lose some. It was about the same way in camping.

Weather forecasts hardly ever deterred us from making a camping trip. On one particular trip, we should've obeyed the meteorologist and stayed home.

It was bright and sunny when we left on Saturday morning for Oregon, Illinois. I made sure, as always, the first-aid kit was fully supplied, the repair-tool kit was readily available, and flares and some ropes were in the baggage. I always carried two clean bath towels tucked in the corner of the car trunk for emergencies.

That habit started way back when I donated a couple of beach towels to several people who were injured in an auto accident and waited for an ambulance to arrive.

That evening in camp, the sky was beautiful and we enjoyed our campsite on a hill overlooking a fifty-foot-deep valley.

A large group of Boy Scouts filled the valley with their tents. It was a pleasure to see them play and sing all evening long.

In the morning it looked like rain. Our daughter, Cindy, reached the age of becoming a lady, and soon she needed some protective sanitary wear. The nearest store was ten miles away. We left the two boys at camp while Betty, Cindy and I went drove to town. We purchased our needs and hurried back to camp.

When we got back, it rained and rained. The valley flooded, water rushing in at more than six inches a minute. I immediately grabbed the rope from the car to help lift those who were climbing out from the fifty-foot-deep valley. Some scouts tried to retrieve their possessions in the rising water, but the scout leader yelled "Leave it." They held hands and formed a chain as they walked up the hill and out of the valley just in time.

By the time the last boy was safely out of the valley, the

water had flooded the prairie where we stood.

All their possessions were lost. The picnic tables and the fifty-five-gallon garbage drums floated away.

A tow motor arrived in a short while and made a new roadway for them to leave. By late afternoon, the water had receded completely, leaving a layer of muddy silt all over the grass. We were alone after all the others left. We saw spoons, forks, and other utensils protruding all over through the thick mud.

Then I thought if the rain came during the night, without any light and no time to dress or find their way in the dark, what a tragedy that would've been.

I looked in the newspapers for an article referring to that terrible incident, but found none.

During the 1970s, camping was a popular way to go. It was

during the Vietnam Confrontation. While driving to and from campgrounds, we passed many hitchhikers, men and women, along the highways. That did not appeal to me. At rest stops some travelers placed signs on the table saying, "Need money for gas," or, "Need money for food." It was difficult to determine who had legitimate needs until seeing their fancy vehicles nearby. Help was always available for those in dire need at the next town.

During that decade, we considered purchasing a lot on some lake for future retirement. With that thought, it meant winding down our camping adventures. The campgrounds were getting too crowded for comfort, with more rowdy people as time passed, and it became more of a hassle at increasingly crowded boat ramps. More and more we thought about some permanent location for recreation.

I had one more camping trip in mind with our boat – the Fox River. I liked a place near Crystal Lake. We camped there several times. This last time we visited, the weather was beautiful; sunny and warm on Saturday and Sunday. We had a lot of fun boating and skiing on the river. It was not crowded.

On Monday morning it was rain, rain, rain. Water came over the river bank and on the ground around our tent and in our tent; about six inches. We slept on air mattresses which were also used for water recreation. They floated around the tent as we laid on them.

I walked outside and saw at least eight twenty-four-inch-long carp floundering in the flooded grass right by our tent. My first thought was to pick them up and throw them back in the river. Well, the sun came out – it was very hot – and the water began to return back to the river.

As this happened, every one of those big carp made flip-flops, side over side with a mechanical motion, all the way across the grass, back over the bank, and back into the river.

I determined they sought cleaner water at its higher level

when the river rose, because the flowing river was very muddy.

My friends asked why I didn't cook some of those carp for a meal. I told them that I did once.

I prepared one by nailing it to a board, covered it with a cloth, and basted it heavily as I fried it. I removed the nails, threw the carp away, and enjoyed the good old basting.

In my experience, carp meat is better when they are caught in clean water.

That was our last camping place... or was it?

Folks asked if we continued camping after that trip. My answer, "Yes." Quite often in Joliet, at St. Joseph's park on many Sunday afternoons since 2002 – mainly for entertainment.

21st Century Mannequins of Beauty

by Carolyn Hill

Albert Einstein wrote, "The most beautiful experience we can have is the mysterious." He most certainly must have had women in mind, for they are enigmatic creatures; personalities who can pull back or emphasize their persona at any given moment. They can be chameleons of physical beauty with no hue of their own; a mystery; and a flat contradiction of reason; both of a simple and yet complex nature.

Even Pharaoh Akhenaten spoke of the importance of how a beautiful woman delights the eye; a wise woman, the understanding; a pure one, the soul. Nothing seems to have changed in this 21st century except, perhaps, man's historic view that women can never be too beautiful or too young.

Influenced by branded advertising, have today's women become something they are not?

Open any women's magazine and you will be whisked into the enchanting world of Advertising, designed to tantalize with endless promises of a new beautiful you. Enticing, colorful ads beckon and tempt like the Gods of ancient Egypt, with sensuous aphrodisiacs and mysterious potions guaranteed to be living in the confines of colorful designer bottles and jars.

It's no wonder the art of advertising can effectively create its own modern-day mannequins of beauty. The ladies are willing...

157

Using creative whims and artistry like a window designer, marketers bombard women with unrealistic goals of "beauty-perfection," and poise. Wherever one looks, from the first burst of youthful essence, through the encroaching borders of the golden age in life, a woman is manipulated to examine her inner self.

It was Earl Puckett, head of Allied Stores, who summed up the world of advertising, "It is our job to make women unhappy with what they have."

How influenced is the inner psyche, by the beauty of the emaciated creature peering back from within a magazine page? Like a chameleon, women are told they must be in constant change. Molded into new combinations of appealing characteristics that excite and delight. Advertisers piece them together at their best on a magazine cover forcing women to camouflage their imperfections, even some that don't exist.

How many of us, that is, separate ourselves from the superfluous advertising world of make-believe when so much in society is based on the youthful essence of beauty?

"At the end of the day, the reflection in the mirror is - the real you," according to scriptwriter Steven de Souza of "Die Hard" fame. It's a type of beauty that speaks to the heart. Not of fickleness or superficiality, but of a dazzling illumination of a modern-day woman wearing many hats; able to discern temporary influences and options to advance her way in life.

And so it is, a secret joy abounds within the 21st century woman for she has cheated time. The state of her life is good, as she grabs back some of what age keeps trying to steal away...the essence of youthful attraction, which has enticed man since the beginning of time.

Winter in My Town

by Diane Perry

The maple trees turn yellow and red in October and the burning bushes burst into color like a fuchsia flower. After all the leaves have fallen creating a blanket on the ground, a smell of Indian summer blows in the soft wind. When the trees are bare, Thanksgiving is just around the corner. Just before Christmas, December 21st, the first day of winter makes its presence known. Winter is one of four seasons, and it is quite different throughout the country. In the Chicago area, we have had blizzards, ice storms, and frigid temperatures in the negative digits which can be beastly. You can hear people contemplate whether the snow or the cold is worse. However, it does have its encouraging moments. That's why people choose to live here.

After a fresh snowfall, the sight of footprints from different animals can be seen. At twilight, deer drink water from the half-frozen creek. The howling of a hungry coyote sounds spooky during the night while being nestled in a warm bed. The sight of a snowy owl eating its prey hides beneath the dry needles of the pine tree. Geese flying overhead through the clouds are talking in unison with each other as a dog barks and runs under them, watching their every move.

Thinking back to my science classes, the molecules outside are packed closer together making the air dense. Looking through this dense air, the crescent moon and stars can be seen by the naked eye. The sounds of a freight train moving down the tracks whistle echoes through the air while the cattails dance from the train's concise breeze. Coming around the bend are bare-naked stick trees, bushes and sculptured evergreen trees covered with powder and glisten like a Thomas Kinkaid picture puzzle. This scene is calm, peaceful, and beautifully serene.

Inside the warming house, a fire is built in the fireplace. The smell outside of the wood burning embraces a warm feeling to invite you inside. After ice skating outside with your turtleneck sweater on, it is time for a break. Your nose leads you to the kitchen where the aroma of hot chili or chicken soup cooks on the burner to satisfy your hunger.

Living in Illinois, there are two options in the winter. One can escape to Michigan on a six-hour drive in the car or head south to Florida on a twelve-hour journey to break out the swimwear and sunglasses. Driving north, the sparkling snowflakes represent tiny stars hitting the windshield. Snow crunches under the tires as the radio plays synchronized with the windshield wipers. Finally, we have arrived.

Getting out of the car, my boots slide on the slippery ice and the cold wind chaps my cheeks. Walking to the mountain the snow is beautifully paved on the terrain as the trails are seen wrapped neatly around all the trees. We race to get our skis. Once our equipment is gathered and ski boots are locked in place, the hat, gloves and scarf are wrapped neatly around our necks. The goggles pop over our eyes as we feel the scrapping of snow under our skis approaching the chair lift. Afterwards, a hot tub is a luxury to soothe the achy, cold soul.

What a delight it is to enjoy a winter sport while putting all the drudgery of cold snow and ice in a positive perspective! People scream with excitement skiing down the hill and using the hockey stop, spraying a wave of icy cold frost on the ground. The chairlift moves skiers above like a clothesline moving laundry at the dry cleaners. Swooshing hips left, right, left to the bottom of the hill to slide in the line then be lifted to the top once again. Whoosh!

Winter has concluded its appearance when I see the Illinois state bird of the cardinal less. The robin has arrived from his vacation destination of Florida as the familiar tweet is heard through the windows. The precipitation of snow has magically turned into rain due to warmer temperatures. The buds on the trees sprouted and daffodils peep their heads out of the ground. The molecules move faster now with the croaking bull frogs announcing spring has finally sprung.

The Blizzard

by Sylvester Kapocius

T he two worst days of the Blizzard of '67 were January 26th and 27th. Those of us who struggled through that storm speak of it often. I had just turned 42 and was employed working at a steel mill located three miles from my house. My shift was from 3 p.m. to 11 p.m. I drove to and from work in a small 1964 Buick Special.

The first morning of the blizzard started out with a light snowfall. After lunch, more wind-powered circles of snowflakes blew around wildly in the air. Because of that, I decided to leave for work extra early. While driving, the radio announced that a serious snowstorm was heading for Chicago. My twenty-minute drive got me to my parking spot right next to the building where I worked at about 2:30 p.m. The blinding snow increased with a very strong wind. The blizzard had started.

I quickly ran to my office, headed right to the boss and told him it was bad outside. The building had no windows so he went out to look and hurriedly ran back, grabbed a phone and made some calls. Radio warnings prompted the dismissal of employees. The lack of workers forced shutdowns in all production departments except our maintenance department. Two women who worked in our office saw they would not be able to drive home in the storm. A huge, coil-carrying lift truck came from the truck department and pulled up to the door of our building. One woman got on and sat next to the driver, the other stood on the step of the vehicle. Both were driven out of the plant to a tavern close by. That was all I knew. Three bosses from my office lived in Indiana. Somehow, they all arrived at the same tavern. They all slept there on the floor overnight. We were stranded.

My superintendent of maintenance occupied a desk four cubicles from my work area. He piled some furniture together to work on. His home was on the far north side of Chicago. The plant utilities foreman was nervous all night long, check the plant's basic needs. About eight machinists were stuck at their stations without work. All the production departments were shut down except the melt shop; that is where the main problem existed.

Tons of melted steel in the pot could not be poured because no help was available to perform the next function in the operation; we could not shut down the melting metal. It would solidify, and the welders' torches would be needed to cut apart that cold steel, piece by piece. That would take three days, then many hours to fire up again. That would be too costly. The melt shop foreman and a couple of his men monitored the situation.

Marv was a first-shift maintenance planner and scheduler, and I worked the second shift, doing the same job. The third-shift man could not get to work because of the blizzard. Marv and I worked the communication system in our office. The foreman on duty was reached either by landline or through our hand-helds. The storm caused us to work twelve-hour shifts.

A railway ran close to Marv's house a mile away, so he was

able to get home after work by walking on the elevated track embankment. The strong wind up there kept the snow shallow. HE brought lots of food for many of us, since the vending machines emptied fast.

My second shift was boring, no communication, no action whatsoever. My office was on the second floor of the maintenance building. A balcony outside our office overlooked all the machinery and equipment necessary to correct problems throughout the entire plant. The building was two blocks long with a single roof. The Calumet River ran parallel to it just one-hundred feet away.

From the balcony, I observed the machinists were idle because of the storm's shutdown. The first night of the storm, I mingled with the men at their machines. I was also well-acquainted with some who worked there. Right around 2 a.m., a huge rate the size of a full-grown cat came through the wall and sneaked into the area in search of food and warmth. Our presence frightened it and it ran back to the river bank.

Two guys devised a rat trap for its return. They got a stick with food scraps tied to it, which held up one end of a heavy board twenty inches from the floor. A fifty-pound weight was placed on the board. Well, the waiting game was short-lived. The rat came back, snatched the food, the heavily-weighted board dropped and smashed half the rat's body. It dragged itself out through the wall and into the dark, leaving a bloody trail on the concrete floor.

Marv relieved me. I walked out of the gate and along the rails to the highway. Ruts left by the truck's were my path toward

165

home; about three miles. To reach my house from the highway, I crawled past two houses from the road.

At home, I got a shovel and dug out a lot of snow around the house. I called my daughter, Cindy, out to pose for a picture next to a six-foot-high pile of snow.

On the second day of the blizzard, after lunch, I dressed heavily for work. On each foot I placed some paper between each of two pairs of socks. I also placed some newspaper between a wool shirt and a thin sweater. I had on a wool hat, a heavy jacket with a woolen scarf, ear muffs, and wool gloves as I began my three-mile trek to work. It was sunny and bright. I walked in the truck ruts left in the snow. As I got to the intersection of 127th and Halsted Street, a helicopter landed there, the front facing the tavern on the northeast corner. It was so close to me, I got lost in the flurried gale of snow from its props.

A pregnant lady who endured the night in the tavern was brought out by the paramedics, placed in the copter, and rushed off to St. Francis hospital in Blue Island. The following day, the newspapers wrote about that incident.

From there I walked down Halsted to 134th Street onto the Calumet River bridge. I passed at least six abandoned vehicles zig-

166

zagged across both lanes on my way. What I saw next was sad. A semi-truck had stalled, with open-slatted sides showed cattle inside freezing to death. That incident also became news the next day. Not a single soul was seen anywhere. I had one more block to walk before turning eastward toward the gate to my workplace. I thought I had it made. A large open field came into view, along with a slight breeze.

I fretted at what I saw ahead. Snow two- to three-feet high for six blocks to the gate of my workplace. No road in sight; nobody anywhere. I thought I should've used the same route as yesterday. Nobody was in sight; I felt like the only person on Earth. The road was not visible. I saw the gate house and aimed for it. I punched my strong legs through the snow with each step. At about the halfway point, I took a long rest, and actually thought about giving up. This wasn't possible.

From days past, I remembered the saying: "A chain is only as strong as its weakest link." I knew I was at my weakest link, but not ready to give up. I forced myself to continue. Within a few hundred feet of the gate I stopped again to rest. I perspired terribly in my clothing. My eyes only saw colored swirls. I was dizzy and almost passed out from the lack of energy. I felt stupid when I reached the gate.

The gate guard said to me, "I don't believe it's you, Lenny, you better show me your pass."

An engineer by the name of Chris, who was also at the gate house, said to me, "An hour ago I saw a small, black dot on the snow

167

as I looked through the window. Then, half an hour later it got larger. As I watched it, minutes later it became alive, the I saw it was you."

During the blizzard our cars were parked along the buildings, now the huge snow drifts covered them. It was a pick-or-miss game to find my vehicle buried beneath the snow.

As days passed, icicles ten inches round and six feet long hung from the building's gutter fifty feet above the ground. One melted, loosened, then fell on a car parked next to the building, causing some damage. Vehicle damage was not covered by the steel mill. We were warned not to walk near the buildings on account of the falling ice.

Two weeks went by and all operations in the mill went back to normal. We who covered the emergency caused by the blizzard were thanked by our superiors and I found a slight increase in my following paycheck.

Some people had become panicky during the days of the storm. Store shelves emptied quickly, some hoarded food, and families with small children got worried as no milk or bread was available for several days on account of late deliveries to the store.

It was a miserable, 29-hour situation. Wind gusts were up to 53 miles per hour. Damage in the Chicago area was estimated at $53 million, and, sadly, 26 people died as a result of the storm.

No More Running

by Carolyn Hill

I can't believe how blindness in spirit once foreshadowed what God was apparently waiting for. The three-letter word, "yes." For me, that commitment proved to be a seven-day proposition I wasn't ready for.

How many times I've thought, "I'm a good person." Then I would let go of God's hand, to continue in the way of the world in believing my journey of faith would remain intact. I didn't see the wisdom of doing His will. My life was good. Because of that, I thought I was reaping the good Lord's favor. That personal opinion regarding what faith entailed was the problem. I never allowed myself to step back and imagine what does being a Christian mean. ... After all, I believed I was.

Did you ever sense when something's not right? Why couldn't I feel the emotion of what it meant to walk in a way that pleases God? When God left it up to me to open the door and invite Him in, I wasn't sure I wanted to live His way. I wasn't ready to handle a life of biblical obedience, (which Hebrews 2:1-3 speaks of), yet I yearned for something which would lead me when I didn't know where to go.

That Christ-exalting faith that brings answers to prayer was apparently on its way, but the learning curve was shattering, yet gloriously effective. Saying "yes" to Christ's invitation would no longer be in doubt. God used an unforeseen circumstance and time to teach me about gratitude. It was a two-edged sword that pierced my soul with anguish that allowed me to see a truth I kept running from. I knew I would be the day's prey in a predator's sadistic hunt for control.

And yet, even with my world-weary attitude, God showed me His love and gave me protection, while delivering me from a final resting place in some forest preserve and a remote hole in the ground.

Why am I so sure?

I remember asking for rescue in an emotional whirl of fear. "Oh God no, please no. Please don't leave me, I don't want to die." If my life was to end at 25, I wanted help to get through those ending seconds. As I stood under the corner lamplight, I remember the soft whisper, of a gentle breeze as if directing my senses to a way out, so calming, so reassuring. If God existed - if His words were not dead - if the Bible is truth, I was about to find out about the deity, whom I had never seen nor heard.

And I did. The Potter who created me defined Himself. Though I was brought to my knees and humbled, I later recalled the truth of Proverbs 3:5, "Trust in the Lord with all your heart and lean not on your own understanding." I guess you could say, God showed His true colors and did indeed walk-the-talk of the written word. His invisible spirit became real to me... and I felt the humanity of His love.

In reflection, rarely does each precious gift of 24 hours

change our lives into terms of mere seconds or life-threatening drama. I remember the Crime Beat reporter told me, "You were very lucky."

Was I?

That statement will be forever embedded in my mind. Is "luck" a shaped probability to the extent to which we can control events that affect us in a favorable or unfavorable manner? Was that night a random coincidence with no apparent connection? Or did fate, if it exists, positively decide my course, as God's way of remaining anonymous?

In the dwindling seasons of my life, I have grown in my thinking since that misty spring eve. Occasionally I wonder, if that night had not happened, would I have continued through life with lukewarm beliefs? I'll never know...

Why?

Three little letters. I gratefully said "yes."

A New Birth

by Diane Perry

As Sara walked in the office, she sifted through the stack of papers which were left in her bin. "Why wasn't this proposal typed and sent out?" She fired out angrily as she frowned.

I replied nervously, "Ted said to wait until next week because the client will be out of town."

Sara had shown volatile behavior since I had known her. When she walked in the room, she had a tendency to upset me because her emotions were like a tumbleweed blowing erratically through a wind storm. I never knew how to communicate with her because she answered in a sarcastic or abrupt manner.

One day as I walked through the office, I saw Sara sitting at her desk crying hysterically. I wanted to console her or ask her what was the matter, but I hardly knew her. I felt like she either didn't like me, trust me or wanted nothing to do with me.

Two months later, I discovered Sara wasn't at work. I finally asked my co-worker, Roxanne, "Where's Sara? I haven't seen her in a while."

Roxanne answered, "She has been out on Family Leave. She was diagnosed with colon cancer. She has gone through surgery and has been receiving chemotherapy treatments for a couple of months now."

"Oh, I hope she will be okay?" I answered.

Sara, a woman in her sixties, was a tall, physically fit and ambitious individual. She was always eating grapefruit or other healthy foods when I saw her. Also, she walked the stairs daily once she arrived at work. When she climbed the stairs to the eighth floor, she always said it felt good while breathing heavily. I often heard how intelligent she was and that she received her pilot's license after attending classes for a year.

It was September now and Sara came to visit us at the office. She was very humbled and dressed casually. I complimented her, "Sara, you are looking good."

She replied reluctantly, "Oh really? Thank you."

One month later, Sara finally returned to work. She was so nice. Her personality did a complete turnaround as she stood taut like a sunflower reaching for more light and positive reinforcement. Finally, she let me into her life as we talked about music, spirituality and political matters. What a delightfully intelligent person she was as I embraced her to be my friend. Glancing at my phone, I received a friend request from her on Facebook. I enthusiastically clicked the "confirm friendship" button.

At the office, Sara saw another co-worker as she burst out in song, "Roxanne, you don't have to put on that red light. Those days are over." And the three of us all giggled and were enlightened by the moment. Sara finally saw me for who I was.

Sitting down for lunch one day she confided in me. "I have

173

stage three colon cancer. If it comes back it will be stage four, and it will be the end of my life."

I said, "You will be fine. It's good you came back to work to be with friends and to get on with your life," as I patted her hand. "I will pray for you."

She said, "If you don't see me one day, that means I have retired."

As time went on, I treasured the conversations Sara and I had. We always seemed to be on the same page with religion and politics. One day, Sara did not show up for work. I was told that she did not retire, but passed away. It was bitter sweet. I was saddened she passed away, but so happy we had become friends. Her thunderstorms of rain were washed away from my memory and her sunshine and funny moments will live with me forever. What a wonderful rebirth of Sara!

Baseball Season

by James Pressler

I can't prove it, but I am sure my conception was the result of some high spirits after the Chicago Cubs swept the St. Louis Cardinals in a weekend doubleheader. However, I do know that by the time I understood the world around me, my mother took me to Wrigley Field to see the Cubs whenever possible. I was a little tyke learning about baseball from the 1969 Cubs. Yes, those Cubs. The Heartbreak Kids. But that's another story.

When baseball season started, Mom got some tickets and we saw what our Boys in Blue brought that season. Before the ivy had turned green, my mother, brothers and I would already have a game under our belts. She always got tickets in the upper deck, first-base side, to have a clear view into the Cubs dugout. Santo and Banks at third and first were her favorites. I sat on her lap and watched her fill out the program, and she showed me the proper way to write down the game. I couldn't even read, but I saw how Mom loved every moment, and how she wanted to share this with her children more than ever.

The first game she allowed me to record on my own was a May game against the despised Cincinnati Reds. I was six and had the worst handwriting, but I diligently tracked every batter, every swing, every hit, error and stolen base. She watched my work, but spent most of the time protecting me from the threat of a foul ball. When the Reds pulled a double-switch in the eighth inning, I scored it perfectly. I could feel her pride, and it made me want to do even better.

After my parents' divorce, the games became different. Those outings became part of her weekend with the kids once school was out. My Cubs weren't the same either. They had become big bats and weak pitching, so we never knew what to expect. Dave Kingman might hit a 480-foot home run clear across Waveland Avenue or strike out to end the inning – usually the latter. But for all the stress from our separated family, financial problems, and all the troubles looming on the horizon, for those three hours we sat in the upper deck, first-base side, and ignored the world while watching the game.

When my mother's work took her from Chicago to Los Angeles, I became a baseball commuter. I visited her for a few weeks in the summer, hopefully when the Cubs played the Dodgers. The baseball season is not very compromising, so it didn't always work out. However, life changed and we had to change with it. I watched games at Dodgers Stadium in Chavez Ravine, seeing fans cheer for Tommy LaSorda and trying to understand the odd habits of the Dodger fans and baseball in the sweltering July heat. I would score the games as usual, but now the Cubs were the away team. Life was changing, and I had to adapt.

Life in Chicago changed as well. During college I became, among other things, a Bleacher Bum. No longer in the upper deck, I sat in the sun, drank my beer, and scored the game from the opposite side of Wrigley. I never drank beer there until I went to the bleachers, but there I was with a beer, cigarettes, and a program. When Cubs outfielder GlenAllen Hill hit a 500-foot home run against the Brewers that hit a rooftop across Waveland Avenue, I thought of sitting with Mom, seeing Dave Kingman do the same thing. But it wasn't the same. I was in the bleachers, and Mom was in Los Angeles.

Many years later, when Mom finally returned to Chicago, we got a few games in, but everything had changed. I showed her the fun of the bleachers and she enjoyed the experience, but still preferred her upper-deck view. I scored the game but now worried about a home-run ball flying at us. Mom's years showed now, so I protected her. She did have a beer with me in the blazing August heat, but just one. Time was catching up with her.

Not too long afterward, her health deteriorated. The walk from the parking place to Wrigley wasn't practical, the heat of the bleachers now dangerous. Her mind lost traction trying to understand the world around her. However, when we went to Wrigley, a lifetime of memories came back, if just for those three hours.

The last game we went to was a September game against those despised Cincinnati Reds. I pushed her wheelchair to our seats in the upper deck, first-base side, so Mom could look toward the Cubs dugout at her Boys in Blue. Santo and Banks had been replaced by Bryant and Rizzo, but none of that mattered. We talked, I scored the game, she dozed off periodically, and I guarded her from foul balls. The Cubs didn't win that day, but that wasn't why I wanted to go to that game.

A few months later, my mom told me about how happy she was to be in Wrigley Field and see that wonderful game where the Cubs finally won the World Series, and being rewarded for her 78 years of waiting. That was what her world had become – she saw the game on TV and thought she was there, not even aware that the game was played in Cleveland. I didn't care. In her mind, the world was complete. We wouldn't be going to any more games, but everything had come full circle from when she first took her children to see the Heartbreak Kids of 1969.

It's just a matter of time now. At the beginning of a new season – maybe the next one, maybe the one after that – I will buy one ticket to an April game. I will go to the upper deck, first-base side, take my seat, and secretly sprinkle some of my mother's ashes about the area. It will be nothing fancy, no big to-do or huge cloud of ash (apparently people have done this before and discovered it is very illegal). I'll just push some ashes about so she can always be within view of the Cubs dugout. I will diligently score the game and hope for a Cubs win. A new baseball season will start, with fresh hopes and possibilities. In that way, life still the same. For those three hours, it will always be the same.

Meet The Authors

R. Patrick Brown (rbrowncubs10@outlook.com)

Patrick is married and has six adult children. He and his wife, Rita, have nineteen grandchildren and fifteen great-grandchildren. As of this writing, two new great-grandchildren are expected in early 2018. He enjoys family gatherings of all kinds. He earned a Master of Corrections at Chicago State University. He has had articles published in local newspapers, his church newsletter and the Chicago Police Department "Star Magazine". Patrick, now retired, was a Chicago Police Department Detective; Cook County Juvenile Probation Officer; and Paraprofessional Educator (Teacher-aide). He also spent two years in the U.S. Army. Since retiring from his position as a Teacher-aide, he began making handmade crosses from horseshoe nails and colored wire. He joined The New Lenox Writers' Group in 2015, where he hopes to continue honing his skills as a writer. He has written stories and poems that have been published in *The Place We Call Home* and *Troubling Times* for the New Lenox Writers' Group. Patrick is presently writing a book about his life as a police officer.

Shannon Carroll (scarroll178@gmail.com)

Shannon Carroll is a student at the University of Illinois at Chicago. She will be graduating in the Fall of 2019 with a Bachelor's Degree in Psychology and Criminal Law and Justice. Ironically, she is not a mystery writer. She writes fantasy — but beware, the story included in this anthology is no ordinary fairy tale. This tale is violent and haunting. Read on at your own discretion. Stories are like the forest: you must explore them at your own risk.

Awesome Angie Engstrom (<u>angie@angieengstrom.com</u>)

 Humans make life too hard. Awesome Angie Engstrom brings simplicity to the complex issues of business and personal life. Her work as a Landscape Designer and Contractor, Professional Organizer, Elite Athlete and Fitness Professional, along with navigating extraordinary parenting challenges has led to a unique mastery of simplicity promoting well-being that has manifested into an incredibly entertaining and enlightening message that has impacted thousands of lives. Awesome Angie inspires everyone; her practical knowledge and profound personal insights exude contagious energy that inspires self-leadership and change. She is a rare blend of visionary, designer, and coach with the ability to speak to her truth, while touching the wisdom of our hearts. There is an unshakable mission in Awesome Angie's soul to instigate change, empower, and impact others to achieve more in less time so that they can live their life on purpose for greater productivity and play. Awesome Angie is the best-selling author of two books, *Overcoming Mediocrity* and *The One Thing Every Mom Needs To Know,* all found on Angie's website at <u>www.AwesomeAngie.com</u>. Through lessons learned from this story and many others, the Achieving More business seminars, workshops and coaching programs were developed. You can learn more at www.GettingYourselfUnstuck.com, including a free download to get you started. Follow her along on major social media channels at AwesomeAngieEngstrom. Awesome Angie lives in Downers Grove, Illinois with her husband, Mike, son, Michael, and schnauzer, Austin. She is known in her community as Awesome Angie because she honors the awesomeness in you.

Carolyn Hill (thatsthestory3@comcast.net)

Carolyn has worked as a columnist for the Joliet Herald News/Chicago Sun-Times media, earned a MFA in creative writing from Connecticut's Charter Oaks State College and the Institute for Writers, contributed political commentary to the Western Journalism Center, and used both writing craft and business skills successfully in a three-year project for the USPS, culminating in the written testimony before a Congressional Sub-Committee hearing in Chicago, Illinois.

Sylvester Kapocius (manus1010@comcast.net)

In his youth, Sylvester enjoyed gymnastics and swimming; his friends called him Sailor because he swam like a fish. He served in World War Two with the Lion Four Navy group in the Pacific. He was discharged at 21 with the rank of Gunners Mate Petty Officer, Third Class. Afterwards he worked several jobs – good and bad – until his retirement. A Navy friend showed him a fifty-page manuscript he wrote about their time, saying he could never be part of the hush-hush generation. Sylvester was convinced he had to do something about it, and he joined the New Lenox Writers' Group. Now, he says his writing will be continuous as long as he can loosen those caged-in memories.

Kenn Kimpell (kibblesandquips@gmail.com)

Kenn Kimpell is a Chicagoland writer, having studied Creative Writing at Illinois State University in Normal, Illinois, who dreams the San Franciscan sun. He evocatively explores mental health and illness with creative nonfiction, and in intertwining works in progress: *The Circus* and *The Faults In Our Mind*. In his free time he pretends to write, or lies about, or complains about not writing enough. His dating-profile likes are: bacon, beef jerky, David Foster Wallace, and the Blackhawks. His dislikes are, in descending order of severity: *The Last Jedi*, those hypothetical kids on his hypothetical lawn, and communism.

Colin Kirchner (mailto:uuspirit@outlook.com)

Colin Kirchner is a professional mental health counselor who works with families, couples, and individuals in the south suburbs of Chicago. He has composed and delivered over a dozen lay sermons at the Unitarian Universalist Community Church of Park Forest, with titles such as: *My Search for Unicorns, We Are All One* (talking about racism), and *Life is a Party*. He is a proud father and seeker of truth. In his spare time, you can find him walking through a forest preserve, playing with his dog, and gaming with friends.

Marlene Lees (mandlstreet@yahoo.com)

Marlene Lees is an author, speaker, artist and strategist who constructs unexpected and inspired solutions by means of a multidisciplinary background. She is a graduate Cum Laude in Business Administration, AAS, minor in Marketing from Moraine Valley Community College as well as a graduate Summa Cum Laude in

Interdisciplinary Studies, BA, minor in Speech and Communication from Governors State University. She is the founder of the group, "Women Enrich Lives" where meaningful topics are presented and substantial personal connections are established. She has enjoyed creative writing and her works have been included in *The Mosaic, The Glacier, The Phoenix, the Airport Journal, O'Hare Airport*. She has recently felt compelled to begin writing more earnestly in finding the need to revisit sated concepts in new ways. She has been a reporter, photographer, editor and publisher, and is publishing her first book. Her essay, *The Fourth Stage*, is part of a larger writing she is working on.

Cora Nawracaj (clovemay48@yahoo.com)

Cora continues to be a work-in-progress poet. She has been writing and journaling on and off since she was 11 years old. She enjoys being retired and has more time for reading, writing, visiting grandchildren and friends, doing volunteer work, and riding her bicycle. "Sometimes pieces of poems start in my head when I'm riding my bike. Then, I have to hurry home and get them on paper," Cora comments. She also added, "I really enjoy our New Lenox Writers' Group. Everyone has inspired me with their immense talent through the years. I look forward to reading our next book."

Diane Perry (perry50rt@comcast.net)

Diane has a Bachelor of Arts in Journalism from Eastern Illinois University, and worked as a reporter for the Star Suburban newspapers. In her spare time, she enjoys companionship with her husband Scott, her dog Ashlee, and her cat Jynx. Diane and Scott enjoy travelling, bicycling, snow skiing, and playing guitar together.

Dawn E. Plestina (deplestina@gmail.com)

Dawn shares her writing with the desire to inspire people to reflect. Through that reflection, she hopes her readers take action to create a more positive world. The documentary, *Dying to Teach: The Killing of Mary Eve Thorson*, featured her reflective writing.

James Pressler (jpres96507@yahoo.com)

James is a career economist who uses creative writing as an outlet for his more playful side. He started writing for personal catharsis and growth, but it rapidly grew into a decades-long passion. His storytelling in the voices of children, ghosts and other characters brings new perspectives to familiar themes, with moods ranging from friendly humor to serious observations on the darker aspects of life. Having written short stories and character sketches for several years, James has also penned two novels (*The Book of Cain* and *Small-Town Monster*), which are being shopped for publication.

Jolee L. Price (rjpcomp@aol.com)

Jolee feels that reading and writing intertwine, opening up the sphere of creativity of one's imagination. Fiction is her favorite theme, although she has written a few works of non-fiction and has had essays in both genres published. She attends the group because she wants to be a better writer, and the diversity of her fellow writers is amazing. They offer criticism in a most helpful, not condescending way, and

184

provide tons of encouragement. The support offered is amazing and genuine. She feels that when one of the members has success with the publishing of a book, article or in just getting that first draft done, it is a group success.

Eric J. Stiltner (redraven84.es@gmail.com)

Eric is the younger of two sons and grew up in Romeoville, Illinois. Upon graduating from Romeoville High School in 2003, Eric received multiple awards and certificates in Culinary Arts and would later go on to college in that field. Even though he loved the art of cooking, he knew in his heart that his biggest passion has always been for writing. Eric has been on several mission trips throughout the world to places such as Mexico, Nicaragua and Haiti. He also is an animal lover and loves spending time with his family. Both sports and music have played a key role in his life. Eric was brought up in a Christian household and holds his faith very close to his heart. Anyone who knows him will say that he is a laid-back goofball!

Paula Morris Thomas (thomas17@ameritech.net)

A lifelong resident of the Lockport/Joliet, Illinois areas, Paula was bitten by the writing bug in the late 1980s when she discovered the joy of journaling. Her desire to be a published writer was heightened and honed beginning in November 2006 when she attended her first meeting at the New Lenox Library and met the founder of our literary family, Miles Snyder (deceased). Paula has enjoyed being included as one of the contributors of the three books that have been published by the New Lenox Writers'

Group, and even created the cover art for the first book, *Writers, We*. In February 2017 she published her first solo book of 256 life points and words of encouragement titled *Life of Days*, available on Amazon.com. She is currently working on two more books that will be part of the *Life of Days* series.

Emilia Weindorfer (penguindor@comcast.net)

Emilia is a long-time member of the New Lenox Writers Group. She contributed six essays for the first anthology Writers We published by the group in 2014, and other essays for the subsequent anthologies. The group continues to inspire her with their multiple writing talents. She is retired after twenty-seven years of teaching and ten years as an elected trustee of the Mokena Library Board. She has four beautiful grandchildren. She and her husband Don have been married fifty-four years, and live in Mokena with their beloved rescue dog, Will.

Made in the USA
Monee, IL
07 January 2020